EVERYBODY'S MEDITATION BOOK— A PRACTICAL, EASY TO USE GUIDE

By Jeff Sauber

This book is designed to be the easiest, most accessible book to offer the benefits of meditation to anyone, especially if you're new to the practice, or if you have tried it before and gotten stuck. Over TWENTY different techniques!

First Edition August 2009

Copyright ©2009 Jeff Sauber

This work written, designed and illustrated by the author,
with the exception of the poem
"If" by Rudyard Kipling, first published in
Rewards and Fairies (1910), and is public domain.

ISBN 978-0-578-03336-5

All rights reserved. No part of this work may be reproduced
by any form or by any means, mechanical or electronic,
including photocopying, recording or any information storage
and retrieval system, without express written
permission of the author.

If you wish to contact the author or order additional copies,
please visit www.21centurymeditation.info

and the blog at:
http://everybodymeditate.blogspot.com/

Acknowledgments

Special thanks to Ed Grant, expert on things cinematic, for his impeccable proofreading and support; Renée Russell for listening to me pontificate all too often; my folks, just because; and everyone who made me think there might be an advantage to just sit down shut up, and find myself for a while (but not to all the people who made me feel the need for it), and to you, dear reader, for giving me a chance.

**EVERYBODY'S MEDITATION BOOK—
A PRACTICAL, EASY TO USE GUIDE**

This work offers a series of mental exercises for self-improvement. It is not intended to be construed as any kind of therapeutic modality, nor is it intended to replace any sort of therapy. Nothing in this work should be construed as making any specific health claims, implicitly or explicitly. If you should experience any kind of odd or unusual effects, physical or mental, or negative symptoms or experiences, stop at once, and if necessary, seek qualified advice from a doctor or mental health professional. Be smart, be safe, be well.

Table of Contents

Foreword i
Introduction iii
Chapter 1—What the heck is it? 1
Chapter 2—Your mind 7
Chapter 3—Beliefs and limiting beliefs 13
Chapter 4—What do you want to achieve? 19
Chapter 5—Centeredness 21
Chapter 6—Yin and Yang 25
Chapter 7—Getting started 29
Chapter 8—Relax! 37
Chapter 9—Breathe! 41
Chapter 10—The basic technique 45
Chapter 11—Meditations on the yin side 47
Chapter 12—Meditations on the yang side 53
    Part A—Focusing on externals 53
    Part B—Focusing on internals 63
Chapter 13—Active meditations for awareness and change 69
Chapter 14—Standing meditations,
    Moving meditations, and living meditations 107
Chapter 15—Strategies for keeping your cool 115
"If" By Rudyard Kipling 128
Conclusion 129
Bibliography 131
Index 135

List of Meditations

Simple Relaxation Technique 37

Meditation 1—Breathing 45

Meditation 2—Emptying your Mind of Sounds and Words (Yin) 47

Meditation 3—Emptying your Mind of Imagery (Yin) 49

Meditation 4—Clearing your Mind of Bodily Sensations (Yin) 50

FOCUSING ON EXTERNALS

Meditation 5—Focus on an External Sound (Yang) 53

    Meditation 5 (Variation)—Focus on OM (Yang) 55

Meditation 6—Focus on an External Sight (Yang) 56

Meditation 7—Focus on a Physical Feeling (Yang) 57

Meditation 8— Focus on an External Smell (Yang) 58

FOCUSING ON INTERNALS

Meditation 9—Focus on an Internal Sound (Yang) 60

Meditation 10—Focus on an Internal Sight/Visualization (Yang) 62

    Meditation 10 (Variation A)—A Picture 63

    Meditation 10 (Variation B)—Colors 64

    Meditation 10 (Variation C)—Picture and Color Combined 65

Meditation 11—Focus on an Internal Feeling (Yang) 66

PERSONAL CHANGE

Meditation 12—Focus on an Affirmation, Mantra, or Prayer (Yang) 69

    Meditation 12 (Variation A)—Repetition 72

    Meditation 12 (Variation B)—Casual Repetition 72

    Meditation 12 (Variation C)—Meaning 73

    Meditation 12 (Variation D)—Prayer 73

Meditation 13—Focusing on a Visualization for Change (Yang) 73

Meditation 14—Focus on a Mirror Reflection (Yang) 77
    Meditation 14 (Variation A)—Mirror..77
    Meditation 14 (Variation B)—A Warm Smile..78
    Meditation 14 (Variation C)—A Confident Gaze..78
Meditation 15—Expanding Peripheral Vision (Yang) 78
Meditation 16—Focus on a Feeling as a "Resource State" (Yang) 80
Meditation 17—Chakra Meditation (Yang)..84
Meditation 18—Emptying Your Mind (Yin)..89
    Problem Solving, Sleep, Intuition, Empathy, Telepathy, Psychometry 93-95
Meditation 19—Guided Visualizations (Yang) 95
    Meditation 19 (Variation A)—Relaxation and Insight......................................98
    Meditation 19 (Variation B)—Developing Skills 101
    Meditation 19 (Variation C)—For a Specific Event 103
Meditation 20—Standing Techniques..109
    Meditation 20—Upright 110
    Meditation 20—Horse Stance 111
    Meditation 20—One Leg 111

    And other applied techniques found throughout.

Foreword

Accessibility.

In one word, that's what this book is all about.

Meditation is an invaluable tool, and this is born out by the fact that it exists in one form or another in every culture and every corner of the world. It's practiced in many different ways, and for many different goals. And when it's done right, it works.

It doesn't take long to get started, and a person can begin to get practical results pretty quickly, but it can be difficult to track down the way that's just right for you.

What I've attempted to do here is to present a variety of techniques, over 20 in fact, in a way that anybody can rapidly find the techniques that are best for them. I think that no matter who you are, chances are that you'll find one or more practices in here that feel good and work well for you. There are meditations for inner peace & calm, awareness, and even personal change. And because a lot of people today are looking for ways to deal with life's difficulties, I've included additional information and techniques for dealing with those difficulties that have worked for me, and are generally recognized as effective.

This work is by no means comprehensive, and I am by no means an expert. I have been an explorer and a practitioner for a long time, and I wanted to share things that have given me and my friends great results and gotten me through some tricky times. There are some people for whom meditation is the biggest thing in their lives, and there are others for whom it's not a big part, just a useful little one, and both sorts of people are achieving what they want. My hope is that this little work allows you to take what you need.

If you're just looking for some quick, appealing practices to help you focus better, or deal with stress, I am confident you can find them here. If you want these kinds of practices to be a major part of your life, I hope this little tome will be a convenient starting point too.

In order to make it accessible, I've avoided most of the jargon. I've extracted the techniques from their cultural cradles, and organized them in a logical fashion. I think each one stands well on its own, but they also can follow a logical progression. And since everyone's different, I've got a nice variety of approaches, so that for every reader, there's something sure to appeal. And since religion and philosophy is a personal matter, I've avoided that for the most part. In the few places I've touched on it, I've tried to give everyone fair representation (apologies if anyone feels I've failed to represent them!). Regardless of what your personal beliefs are, you should be able to find some approach here that will complement it nicely, should you choose to go in that direction.

You will also find a little bit of me in this book. While I've distilled the techniques down to their essential essences as I understand them, I've endeavored to flavor much of this work with personal experiences and observations, as well as my understanding of the mechanics and psychology involved. I've been an artist, a graphic designer, a competitive fencer and athlete, a teacher of various subjects, a hypnotist and a Master Practitioner of Neuro Linguistic Programming, and you'll find these things have all guided my awareness. I hope this will make the entire work both entertaining and edifying.

We live in a stressful world. Our everyday life offers plenty of ways to get overwrought, drained, and confused. There's no shortage of ways push you to the end of your rope. This book is an attempt to balance things out.

Without further ado—Let's GO!

Jeff Sauber

Happily Lost in Space 11/2008

Introduction

I was talking to a guy at a hypnosis practice group the other night. He didn't know anything about hypnosis, but he was looking for any kind of technology that would help him focus better and achieve more in his high-stress job, while keeping the stress from spilling over into the rest of his life. I'm a hypnotist, and one of the guys running the event. I also happen to have a lot of experience—decades, probably—with meditation.

Anyway, the guy tells me he's been attending talks with some of the top motivational speakers, and he feels he's really got a lot out of them.

"Yeah?" I say.

"Yeah!" He answers.

"And you know, most of them talk about how important meditation is."

"Yeah?" I say.

"Yeah!" He answers.

"And they credit a lot of their success to their own daily meditation."

"Yeah?" I say.

"Yeah!" He answers.

"Cool!" I say.

"Yeah!" He answers. Then he adds, "so, how do you do it?"

Now I don't know which gurus he was listening to, and I can't speak for what works for them, but I can tell you what I've been doing, and what's worked for me. And over the years, I've found that a few minutes of practice has worked wonders for me and even helped me survive against seemingly insurmountable circumstances.

You see, in meditation, you give yourself a little time to separate yourself from all those strings and wires of stress, emotion and obligation that cause so much stress. It can help you renew your sense of who you are, separately from what's being demanded of you by others or yourself. It can give you a chance to get a new perspective on your situation. It's relaxing and refocusing at the same time. No doubt his gurus recommended meditation for centering one's self, while helping to redefine one's goals.

Chapter 1
What the heck is it?

Oof. What the heck is meditation? I was born in the early 60s; I was a kid in the 70s. In those hazy, colorful decades, meditation was just something in the air. It was the incense smoke left behind when conformity was thrown into the fires of the counterculture. Meditation? It just was. It was something that helped you. It was a way of life. It was a way out. A way in. The solution. Something exotic—the secret of Hindu Yogis and Shaolin monks. It brought wisdom. It brought eternal life.

Did any of those answers help you? I thought not.

I got my first taste of meditation from a buddy in elementary school, who was very taken with the hippie ethos. It went like this: "OK, clear your head and tell me the first word that comes onto your head."

I took a moment, closed my eyes, and thought of empty space.

"Space." I said.

"That's your word forever, now. For the rest of your life you'll meditate on the word 'space.'"

Waitaminit, I thought, I didn't want the word "space" for the rest of my life! I wanted something strong, powerful. I didn't want empty space, like the place in the closet behind the sneakers! What a stupid exercise!

And that was the last of my formal exercises in meditation for a long time.

Or maybe not, really.

At the same time, I loved to draw, and could spend hours, even days, on a single picture. I went to an art school on Saturdays where we sat and drew or painted, for four hours at a time, with a five minute break every half hour. We worked mostly in silence, because there was nothing that needed saying, and I loved it.

I also loved reading, and tore through every science fiction book I could get my hands on. I went to summer camp, but I wasn't very athletic at the time, and since most of the activities there were sports, I had a lot of time to explore nature and to read, and read I did. Roughly a book a day. My record was three paperbacks in one day.

And when I was a little older, I often came home from school, threw an LP on the stereo, and zoned out on the couch while my imagination transported me wherever it wanted to take me.

Was any of that meditation?

Isn't meditation some exotic import of the East? I mean, there have to be all sorts of formalities, right? You have to sit a certain way, you have to sit on certain special things in certain special positions, burn special incense, and chant stuff out loud, right?

Well, yes, and no.

Meditation is a function of the mind, and as long as you have a mind, and you do, you have everything you need to start.

Sure, there are certain formal schools and styles of meditation, probably millions of them, and some are probably culturally closer to you than you'd imagine, but the bottom line is that they all aim to teach people to get to the *state of meditation*. It can be a little difficult to say exactly what the *state* of meditation is, since different people achieve it differently, and also experience it differently. But most meditative states have in common a few things: mental focus, calmness, a feeling of being centered in yourself, and of being totally connected in the moment, so that past & future concerns can be put aside for a period of time. Most important, all of that is being consciously controlled by the practitioner.

Most formal styles of meditation include certain customs, usually ones that come from the cultures and environments that these styles of meditation were evolved in. For a person who has grown up within that environment, these customs can make the practice more comfortable and relevant. For a person coming from another culture, these customs can be helpful, or an obstacle. For example, any meditation coming out of a religious tradition may be difficult to fully appreciate it you don't know the conventions and symbolism particular to that religion. A meditation based on a Christian prayer, a Jewish psalm, or a Tibetan mantra can only be of limited use if you don't understand what the symbols or deities represent. And then there are customs. Japanese Zen meditation is traditionally done sitting in *Seiza*, a traditional way of sitting in Japan, but which can be very difficult, to the point of distraction, to an unfamiliar Westerner. If you choose to explore more deeply, you may find a particular school or style that appeals to you, and be introduced to such things. In that situation, such knowledge and customs can help to deepen your experience.

In nearly any dictionary you look at, you'll find the definition of meditation as "extended thought or contemplation," so it's natural that every tradition that ponders the deeper questions, and even the questions of everyday issues, has made use of meditation practices of some sort. Here's a very, very brief overview of some of the religions and cultural sources commonly associated with meditation:

Hinduism—Indian in origin, Hinduism is amongst the world's oldest religions, and according to historians, has always placed emphasis on meditation. Hinduism is considered to be a religion, but can also be considered to be a philosophy. One of the key elements of Hindu thought is the evolution of the soul over many lives. Meditation is one of the tools to achieve refinement of the soul, as well as a tool for deeper understanding of scriptural material. In some traditions, meditation is also used to encourage the favor of a particular deity to change one's situation. Over the course of thousands of years, and with so many different deities and philosophies included in it, a bewildering variety of approaches to meditation have arisen. Some were very severe, and included austerities like fasting and self-punishment.

Buddhism—Also Indian in origin. Like Hinduism, Buddhism is a philosophy as well as a religion. Buddhism was founded by Siddhartha Gautama around 500 BC. His goal was to find a method to free peoples' spirits from the suffering that material life can inflict, without going through the extremes of some Hindu practices. Spiritual evolution is also a key element of Buddhist thought, for many of the same reasons as it is for Hinduism. By focusing the mind through meditation, the practitioner aims at separating what is "ultimately, spiritually real" from what is false perception. Buddhism spread throughout the East.

Zen Buddhism—A particular school that developed in Japan from Chinese travelling Buddhists. This school of Buddhism places greater emphasis on meditative experience as the path for enlightenment rather than scriptures or philosophies. Zen perspective focuses very much on discerning the true nature of things, and the self, in everyday life. The Zen practitioners often employ "koans," or paradoxical riddles, to shake loose their accepted perceptions. A koan is a question with no obvious or logical solution. One of the most famous koans is "what is the sound of one hand clapping?" I think the particular aesthetic austerity of Zen reflects that influence of the Japanese culture which nurtured it.

Tibetan Buddhism—Another approach to the Buddhistic practices of self cultivation from Tibet, this belief system synthesized the preexisting Tibetan beliefs and practices with Buddhism. It includes a variety of physical, energetic and ritual practices, and shares the Buddhistic idea of using these practices to liberate one from the illusory sufferings generated by the concerns of the material world. There is also a strong monastic tradition in Tibet that emphasized meditation and spiritual exercises.

Taoism—From China. There is a philosophy of Taoism typified by the works of the ancient (and possibly mythical) philosopher Lao Tzu, as set down in the book *Tao Te Ching*, and by subsequent Taoist scholars. It is somewhat separate from the religion of Taoism, which is more ritualistic in nature. "Tao" means "the way" or "the path." It advocates discerning and following the most natural, moderate way to live with least resistance, or "effortless being." Taoism often advocates "a mind like water." Water flows and adapts to its surroundings, and only becomes stagnant when it ceases to move. Flowing water will gradually erode even the biggest mountains, and similarly, a mind that is not stagnant can eventually overcome its biggest obstacles. The religion of Taoism includes native Chinese animistic beliefs and traditions. Interestingly, while most philosophies place man at the pinnacle under god, Taoism places him within nature, and as a part of it.

Judaism—Judaism also originated in the Middle East, and is another of the world's oldest religions. References to meditation, contemplation, and prayer are found throughout the Old Testament. Some of the traditions of Jewish meditation are related to the Kabbalah, which is a somewhat mystical study of the interrelation of all the things in the universe. One can find practices of reading or reciting scriptural material similar to mantra practices, contemplative meditation upon a biblical theme, and even complex mathematical mind exercises in the study of the Kabbalah.

Christianity—Originated from Judaism in the Middle East, and took strong root all over Europe and the New World. Christianity has a long history of meditation, both intertwined with prayer, which some consider a sort of meditation by itself. Using various forms of contemplation to "know God" and see the truth behind daily things, one can find a meditative tradition throughout the history of the religion. Certain luminaries emphasized meditative exercises, such as Meister Eckhart (German, 13th Century), who took a somewhat mystical approach, urging followers to meditate upon the deeper meanings in scriptural material for a better understanding of both God and nature, and St. Ignatius Loyola (Spanish, 16th century), who advocated a month-long program of spiritual exercises. It also goes without saying that there is a very strong monastic tradition in Christianity that includes prayer and meditation.

Islam—Also originating in the Middle East and spreading throughout parts of Asia and eastern Europe, Islam makes use of meditative prayer. Moslems pray five times a day, in a ritual which employs contemplation, physical and verbal activities, all combined to keep one's focus, and help one maintain a particular state of being. By praying five times a day, that state can be reinforced to carry through most of the waking hours.

Other sources—Virtually every culture on earth has some sort of prayer or meditative tradition to help their followers achieve a deeper understanding of themselves and their place in the world, as well as using meditation as a tool for coping with life's everyday issues.

This book will focus primarily on the practical. If you like, you can use what's offered here as a basis for a deeper exploration into a specific style of meditation that appeals to you, but this book does not intentionally endorse or follow any particular style. Any of the techniques in this book can yield pleasing results with a little regular practice, just as they are, without any additional materials or tools.

To that end, I'm going to use as little jargon and unique terminology, as I can get away with. There are a few Eastern terms I'll use for convenience, and they're all in popular usage, so they won't be difficult to comprehend.

Let's get started.

Chapter 2
Your mind

OK, let's put your mind on the table for a minute, and have a look at it.

Over here is something called the "conscious mind," and over there is the something called the "subconscious mind," (sometimes called the "unconscious mind." The term 'unconscious' really helps to distinguish it from the "conscious" part, but trust me, it's anything but unconscious!).

There's a difference between your mind and your brain. The brain is an organ—easy to identify and define, while your mind is... well, complicated. Your mind, more than your brain, is mostly *you*. Your mind includes all of your, feelings, thought processes, your character, your memories, and everything in between. For simplicity's sake, let's say your mind is most often found inside your brain (even when you're absent minded).

Brain study and anatomy is a subject that can go on for a lifetime. Let's just touch on the most common things we hear about the brain. There are two halves to your brain: the left brain and the right brain. These days you've probably heard all you need to about the two: one side's the creative side, the poet and the feeler and the artist, and the other is the accountant, the mathematician and the file clerk. That's good enough. Let's just avoid divisive descriptions, except to say our practice ought to help balance out the distinctions into one glorious...mind.

So what does the mind do? I mean, you have a stomach, and it processes the food you eat; you have a liver, and it processes the blood; your lungs process air. The mind seems to process like an organ. What does it do?

Foremost, it processes **thoughts**. They come in, they go out, they divide there, multiply there, they die and are born there, and sometimes they just keep rattling around in there, looking for mischief.

Feelings also seem to rumble around in there very much the way thoughts do, and your mind processes them in a very similar way. While we're at it, you've probably noticed that thoughts sometimes beget feelings, and feelings sometimes generate thoughts. Now that's a great thing when it works for you, but rotten when it works against you. Think about it for a minute. A great artist, maybe a poet or a composer, is able to translate feelings into something that he can communicate to others in a way that they can experience what he's feeling, too. Think of Mozart, or Paganini, Picasso or Bob Dylan, Shakespeare, Tupac (or anyone who moves you). If they were able to convey something they felt in a way that you could feel it too, well, that's pretty special, isn't it?

At the same time, strong emotions, improperly handled, can move a person in very different ways, cause them to make themselves miserable, or do things they'll later regret.

It's not just feeling and behavior that's processed by the mind. It's been known for a very long time that the state of mind can affect the body and health. In fact it's been proven in many studies that meditation can positively affect your health, self image, even immune response.

> Scientific research has been validating the mind's ability to influence and heal the body since at least the 1970s. People like the Australian psychiatrist Ainslie Meares, who reported using meditation successfully to reverse cancer, in *The Medical Journal of Australia* in 1976. Meares was also the author of several books on the subject, including his bestseller *Relief without Drugs*, Dr. Herbert Benson of the Mind-Body Medical Institute, part of Massachusetts General Hospital, defined the "relaxation response" in which the deep relaxation of the meditative state enhances physical healing and well being. Dr. Benson is the author of several books, including the groundbreaking bestseller *The Relaxation Response* which was first published in 1975.

The reason the stuff in your brain affects your body has to do with how closely your conscious and subconscious mind act together. While your conscious mind is grappling with your thoughts, awarenesses, and plans, your subconscious is coordinating with your conscious mind to bring you memories and feelings about those thoughts, and expertly handling all the interconnections of mind and body, past and future, all at the same time.

They say the conscious mind tends to handle things in a linear fashion, one item at a time, and can handle a maximum of 7 plus or minus 2 things at a time. Which is to say that you can usually hold about 5 to 9 things in your conscious mind at a time, and it's easier to focus on one thing after another.

Now your subconscious mind is aware of everything that your conscious mind doesn't have time for. The subconscious mind is in charge of handling all your memories, feelings, habits, and instincts. And also *everything else* your body is doing, all the time. Right now, for example, as you read this, receptors in your skin are feeding your mind the air temperature of the room, your ears are picking up sounds that your conscious mind doesn't notice, your various organs are feeding information back into your brain, and your subconscious mind is taking all of this in and responding to it, as necessary, on top of everything else. For example, you're probably not aware of your bladder filling up, until it's about time to empty it. At that point, your subconscious mind will tap your conscious mind on its shoulder, and suddenly bladder status becomes important to your conscious mind. This connection goes both ways—just as your body influences your mind, so does your mind influence your body. If a scary thought, maybe a spooky book or movie, is being processed through your conscious mind, your subconscious will respond as if there's a real potential threat, by pumping up your adrenaline levels and tensing your muscles. So the communication goes both ways—from subconscious to conscious, and from conscious to subconscious. In this way, your thoughts can actually affect your body. Get it?

Another example is this: Take a minute now to imagine you're going to a beach or a forest, and find a quiet place where you can relax, *really* relax. You take a deep breath, and let it go. Now, you begin to allow your muscles to unwind, and your thoughts to slow down. Maybe there isn't much changing in the immediate surroundings, so there's not a whole lot of sensory input for your mind to be aware of, so it, too, can slow down. And that just feels nice, doesn't it? Think about it for a minute, really imagine you're there. Can you feel it? How does that feel?

If you're feeling different from just having read that once or twice, we've already gotten started. And you might have learned a little something: The mind can relax the body and, by imagining you're someplace that relaxes you, can have an effect like the actual experience. Cool, huh?

If that worked for you, fine! If not, don't worry, we're going to cover a lot of different approaches, and this is only one of them. I just wanted to make you aware of the *mind-body* connection. If that mind-body connection didn't work, nobody would have a reason to go to the movies or listen to music!

While we're at it, let's talk about the speed of the mind for a second. Did you know your brain functions at different speeds at different times? I mean, you wake up in the morning and you're still a little groggy. You get a little caffeine in you, and (hopefully) a good breakfast, and you're charged and ready to face the day. During the course of the day, you might get a little faster or slower, based on how close it is to lunch. At the end of the day you're tired, but your friend calls and invites you out to a club, and you have a new burst of energy. You come home exhausted, hit the pillow, and you're out. Tomorrow, it starts again.

Here are the speeds your brain runs (actual mileage may vary):

> **Gamma** (30-100Hz) Super alert! This one was only recently discovered by researchers working with Tibetan monks. It's not known if most people can reach this state without training.
>
> **Beta** (15-30Hz) Uptime, you're wide awake
>
> **Alpha** (8-15Hz) Light meditation
>
> **Theta** (4-8Hz) Trancy, deep meditation
>
> **Delta** (0-4Hz) You're asleep
>
> (Hz stands for Hertz, which represents the number of cycles per second)

It's generally assumed that the higher the speed, the more the conscious mind is at the forefront. At the slower speeds, the subconscious mind comes out to play, and also do its work, including bodily maintenance, which is another reason why meditation and sleep may be beneficial to your health.

Some other interesting considerations about your mind:

YOUR SENSES

You know you have five senses, but did you know that most everybody has a *favorite* sense? Bet you did, even if you never paid much attention to it before. Maybe you've noticed the way certain people are all about the visual: pictures, colors, and shapes, while other people are all about the way something sounds to them, still others are most aware of the things they can do, and the way they feel about things.

For the record, your five senses are: sight, hearing, touch, taste, and smell.

A person's dominant sense is the one that their mind uses most, and there are three that are most common: vision, hearing, and feeling.

Think about it. Some people are always talking about how something *looks* to them, the *shape* of it, how it *colors* their day... Other people might *hear* what you're saying; they know when something *rings* true, it's *music* to their ears... Still others have *a feeling* about something, they like to *do* things, they have a *gut instinct*....

People whose dominant sense is **Visual** usually perceive the information that comes into their brains in terms of pictures, and through pictures & graphics they organize their thoughts. These people may have photographic memories, be able to see things in terms of structures and colors, and organize thoughts & feelings in positions relative to each other.

Auditory people, the ones whose mind interprets everything in terms of sounds, will be extremely aware of tempo and sound and descriptions of things.

Kinesthetic folks are all about how something feels to them, and the actions they take.

If you begin to listen to your friends, you'll start to hear the kinds of words that they use, and the ones they use the most are clues to what senses their mind favors. Mind you, everybody uses all three to some extent, and some people will favor one sense in certain situations and not in others, so it's pretty broad.

You might have noticed I left out smell and taste. These two are the most specific, and so are somewhat less developed in most people. But if you happen to know a chef, a sommelier, or a perfumer, their smell and taste might be much more highly developed than in other people. So there are a few people who sense their world in terms of flavors and scents, but such people tend to be few and far between.

Just for something to think about, did you ever notice that each sense has a particular *range*? In order to taste something, it has to be *in* your mouth. In order to touch something, it has to be *within arm's reach*. You can smell things far away, but you have to be *fairly close* to smell it accurately. You can hear sounds from *fairly far* away, and you can see things that are *very far* away. Interesting, huh?

There are meditation techniques that appeal to each of the senses. Some use sounds, some use sight, and some use feeling, and we'll even talk a little bit about scent and taste.

MOTIVATION

One more thing worth considering: **Motivation**. Maybe you never thought about this before, but if you stop and look at what motivates people, you'll begin to notice that some people get stuff done when there's a reward at the end of it, and others are at their best when they know they have to do it, or else. It's the old carrot and the stick—some horses are motivated to move forward by the promise of moving *toward* a tasty carrot, others are motivated by moving *away from* the potential of getting hit by a stick.

We generally talk about people's motivation as being *toward* or *away from*. Like the sensory modalities, there's a little variation in everybody, but knowing which motivates you the best will help later on when you're using meditation techniques for achieving your goals.

Once you find meditation techniques from this book that you enjoy and want to practice, ask yourself what you want to achieve from them. For example, are you trying to achieve a certain state of being, or trying to get away from an undesirable one? It doesn't have to be overly specific, maybe just something general, like "more inner peace" or "new insights on a situation." **For many people a *toward* goal, like "more calmness and happiness," works better than an *away from* goal** like "getting away from that frustration" or "not being so tense."

Chapter 3
Beliefs and limiting beliefs

It's worth taking a moment to talk about *beliefs* and *limiting beliefs*.

What is a limiting belief? What the heck is a *belief*, to begin with?

First I'll tell you what I *don't* mean when I refer to beliefs in this book. When I talk about a belief here, I don't mean a religion or a philosophy. Those include cultural elements and historical elements, and they often offer explanations for life and the universe. They also offer solutions and insights, too. Sadly, for some people, they can create limitations. I feel this is usually a result of misinterpretations and good things wrongfully applied. That's really not what they were made for.

The beliefs I will be talking about from here on in are the kind of personal beliefs that you have within you about yourself and your surroundings, the kind of beliefs that shape you and your universe. Most people aren't aware of it, but who they are and the world they live in are determined by the beliefs they hold. Those kinds of beliefs are beliefs that a person lives with everyday, and they're so familiar that most folks aren't aware that they're there at all, until they become challenged in some way.

When a person is born, they are open to all sorts of sensations that they will later take for granted. But when we first enter the world, everything we're aware of has equal importance. A baby is as aware of the sound of a voice as he is of the texture of the blanket underneath him, the temperature of the air, the feelings in his tummy, the color of the wall, the smell of his mom, and a million other things. A baby's first job is to figure out which of those sensations is important to be aware of and which isn't. Obviously, things related to his comfort take top priority, along with things related to mom. If you've ever been around really young babies, you can see then reacting to all the things around them. All of that silly baby stuff they do, the looking, touching, and tasting you see them do, is actually the serious work of learning how to make sense of the world he's in. Human babies develop slowly, because it takes a long time to figure it all out!

He learns that some things are "good" and others aren't. Now we adults know that good and bad aren't absolutes, but it's the first classification system that we use when we're born, and it sticks with us. Good and bad are things that we *believe* about the things we know.

As we get older, our experiences will be classified in our minds in many ways, but good and bad will still be an important classification.

Enough baby talk! Let's jump ahead to us as grown-ups. We know what's good and bad. We know what we can do and what we can't. But are we right?

Did you ever know anyone, maybe even yourself, who just *knew* that they didn't like a particular food or an experience, until one day, all of a sudden they did? That feeling you *won't* like something is a *limiting belief*. It's something that you kind of "know," that limits your future behaviors. I can tell you, when I was a kid, papaya fruit was considered super-healthy, and it seemed like it was everywhere. Maybe they said it was good for you, but I hated it! I couldn't think of a worse-tasting fruit—to me it tasted like rotten meat. Then one day, I was on a flight to Australia, and they served a fruit salad on the plane made with Australian fruits, including papaya. I loved it! And I've liked it ever since. I changed my belief about papaya in 10 seconds. Just that fast. Now I love it!

Beliefs are like that. We believe some things to be good and some things to be bad, and what we believe about a thing when we first learn about it will program our future behavior. You can have a single bad experience and it programs your brain for the future: for example, papaya = bad. Every time you see papaya, it sets off the program, and you know papaya is bad. But like any bit of computer programming, it can be replaced by better programming when the time is right. For me, it took a tasty piece of papaya to show me what I was missing.

That's all well and dandy, but fruit salad may not be very important in your life. Here's the thing: the same process that can limit a person's ability to enjoy a particular fruit can limit what they achieve in life. Beliefs shape our world. Everything we think we can do, and can't do, is the result of our beliefs. Oddly enough, the same beliefs that literally shape our world, and free us or trap us, can change as quickly as eating a piece of fruit. What if, instead of eating papaya fruit, the belief had been about learning to play the piano, or getting a better job?

What are your limitations in life? Is there something you'd like to do, but you *know* you can't? Maybe you tried and failed, or maybe you never even tried to being with. If you're lucky enough to live an unlimited life, try to think of someone you know who does allow limiting beliefs to rule their life. Maybe they say something like this:

I want to play a musical instrument, but I have no talent

My life is not in my control

I want to take dance classes, but I'm not flexible enough

Nobody in our family has ever been to college

I don't deserve this

I wish I had a girlfriend, but I'm not good looking

Nobody thinks that way in our part of the country

You have to make compromises in life

You can't always get what you want

I'm afraid of heights

I want to be more successful in business, but I don't seem to have what it takes

I could play ball if only I were taller

You get the idea. Are any of these familiar to you in any way? I don't know about you, but the first question that comes to my mind when I hear these kinds of statements is: "Says who?"

I'll tell you who: you. There's something like a "little voice" in our head that says these things. In fact, this little voice doesn't just tell us these things, it reminds us constantly, and often it's the most strident at the times we're considering doing something we've never done before. And for most of us, we aren't even aware of it, until something brings it to our attention. Until then, they're just things we believe about ourselves. They keep us from achieving, or even attempting to achieve. Some people struggle all their lives against their limiting beliefs, and the internal conflict can annoy, torture, or even ruin their lives.

It's not uncommon to find this kind of struggle at the root of many kinds of addictions and self destructive behavior.

If you were able to eavesdrop on the "little voice" in the head of most of the people you pass on the street, you'd be amazed at the terrible things they're saying—about themselves! Have you ever done that to yourself? Most people talk to themselves in a way they'd never, ever let anyone else talk to them! They also talk to themselves in a way that they'd probably never talk to anyone else. I know you've never done that. Right?

The limiting beliefs sound terrible, you say. Why would our inner mind do this to us? Oddly enough, these limiting beliefs want to keep us safe! *They mean well.* But they can be overprotective. They're limiting us to keep us in a familiar place, our comfort zone, if you will. They want to keep us safe, and try to talk us out of going into new and unfamiliar territory where we may be faced with dangers we've never faced before. Limiting beliefs don't care about the benefits that may be out there, they just want you to be safe. And safe is where you are, no matter what that may be. There's an old saying: "The devil you know is better than the devil you don't."

One of the benefits of meditation is that, when we quiet the mind, or occupy it in some other, similar way, these limiting beliefs become more apparent, and that allows you to examine your beliefs and maybe replace them with better ones.

Not all beliefs are negative. In fact, your perception of the world is basically your collection of beliefs. Some are very basic. Your belief in gravity is proven true every minute of every day. Even if you try to convince yourself against it, you can't. Most beliefs are positive. For example, beliefs in your own abilities give you confidence and charisma. Strong, supportive beliefs open you to grabbing at success, making good decisions and improving your life.

By meditating in a mindful way, you'll become more aware of your beliefs and more able to develop the beliefs that work best for you.

Sometimes you'll hear people talk about *internal dialogue*. It's a funny function of the mind that it tends to run a sort of lecture that keeps reinforcing the beliefs. When you get into any particular emotional state, you'll find there's usually a congruent inner dialogue running, if you just make the effort to be aware of it. Think of the last time you tried something really new and different. Maybe you got nervous, felt your knees trembling and palms sweating, as you did it. Do you remember the words running through your head at the time? Was it "this is easy! I'm going to have fun doing this!" or was it "Oh, boy...I hope I don't screw up!"

Now, you may be wondering, if it's a kind of internal lecture, why is it called an internal dialogue and not a monologue? If you ever stop to examine what's going on at the very borders of your conscious awareness, you'll discover that as the little lecture is going on within you, you're also having an internal reaction to it, usually in the form of feelings or ideas. It's actually the interplay of the two that gives that dialogue the strength to affect your feelings.

As you do the following techniques, you may find that you become more and more aware. I'll also present techniques that you can use to create better self-programming, so you can choose the best possible beliefs for you.

Chapter 4
What do you want to achieve?

One of the most important rules in life is to know where you want to go so you'll know when you get there. You know, there's an old saw that goes: "The important thing is not whether you reach the goal; it's the journey that counts."

Phooey!

If you don't have a goal in mind, you may as well go around in circles.

What that saying refers to, in my humble opinion, is that you have to be open-minded on your journey, because you may be presented with surprises that you'll miss if you're too focused on your goal. However, if you don't know where you want to go, how will you know which direction to move towards? A journey, by its nature, is transformative and enlightening, but it needs a direction.

A sense of direction makes life much more dynamic.

So, with that in mind, let me ask you: *what do you want to get out of this?*

Read through this book. Start with the first technique, or pick a method that you feel moves you, and try it for a while. If it works, see where it leads you, and if you don't feel it is working for you after a reasonable time, say 2-3 weeks, try a different method. At the very least, you'll have learned what doesn't work for you, until you come to the right method. I'll explain what I think each method is good for, but see for yourself.

Here are some goals that bring people to meditation:

Stress relief

Better mental focus

Better self control

Better emotional connection

Improved creativity

Self-development, like changing habits or self-image

Self confidence

Better health

Calmness

Insight

Awareness & sensitivity

Achieving goals

Well that's a start. Do you see your goal on the list? If not, write it in! You'll be amazed what your mind can do for you. When you start moving forward with your goal in mind, you can begin to be aware of other changes and benefits that result from these practices.

Chapter 5
Centeredness

What does it mean to be centered? Well, where are you right now? I mean, you're *here*, wherever here is to you. Maybe in your office, or your bedroom. Your body's here, but how much of your mind is here? How much of your mind even knows you're here?

Some parts of your mind are thinking about where you have to be in the future, in an hour, or a couple of days. There's another part that's remembering things, too. Places you just came from, or things you did, maybe just a few minutes ago, maybe a long time ago. And then, maybe there are the things you should have done, and the places you should have been. On top of all of that, maybe still another part of your mind is thinking about the places you'd like to be right now, maybe have to be, instead of the one place you are. And with every one of all of those thoughts are bits of sensory information—sights and smells and sounds and memories and emotions. Wow! Sometimes you might even forget where you really are right now while you're trying to process all of that stuff.

Getting centered is all about getting your mind to the place where your body is. You know, all of those thoughts, the mental baggage we just mentioned? You can put it down for a while. Just leave it all piled up at the door. I can guarantee that it'll be there waiting for you when you're ready to pick it up again. In fact, if you take a little time to get centered, when you go back to pick all of that stuff up, you may find that you can do it a lot more easily, and you may even find better ways of handling it all.

Another important part of being centered is **getting control of your emotions**, and maybe even getting them out of your way entirely for a little while. Emotions usually arise spontaneously. Emotions give meaning to everything around us, but they don't always offer good strategies for action. Some people seem to be at the mercy of their emotions, and that's a very difficult place to be. If something makes them angry they act out, if they're scared, they react. Human beings are thinking creatures, and allowing emotions to short-circuit the mind's ability to understand and act appropriately can be crippling and very destructive. Someone who always allows their anger to control them might even end up in prison. Some folks control their negative emotion by suppressing them, but that's not a good strategy either. Emotions have a physical component, too, and even if a person doesn't show the emotion, they're still feeling it. Repressing emotions can be bad for a person's health. Like a big bubble of energy, if you push it down in one place, eventually it'll pop up in another. Practicing meditation and getting into the habit of calmness can allow a person to stay more objective in a stressful situation, and maybe see if there's a better way out than reacting emotionally. In fact, people who act out strongly and emotionally usually do so because they feel they have no other options available to them.

Being centered gives you perspective.

I'm going to avoid most of the philosophy that comes along with meditation—it's easy enough to find if you want to look for it, and it may give you some great insights—but you know, a lot of it came about as the result of a person, just like you, getting centered, clearing out his brain for a while and experiencing the everyday in a fresh new way, then thinking about it and writing it down.

If you think about all of the energy you have right now going out in so many different directions, into the past and the future, into all of those feelings and memories and to-do lists, well, you can see why you'd be frazzled. Getting centered is all about bringing all of your energy back to you.

The word "centered," to me, brings to mind a picture of a circle with a dot in the middle, with an even amount of space all around that dot. Kinda static, kinda peaceful. What does the word "centered" make you think of?

Marcus Aurelieus, one of the main voices of the Stoic philosophy, said it very nicely:

> The spherical form of the soul maintains its figure, when it is neither extended towards any object, nor contracted inwards, nor dispersed, nor sinks down, but is illuminated by light, by which it sees the truth, the truth of all things and the truth that is in itself.

You know, from time to time, I've been faced with a great deal of emotional adversity, having my feelings stretched thin by difficulties that were out of my control, by people who were making me feel terrible. Being able to detach my feelings for a bit and take stock of the situation really helped me get through some tough times.

Chapter 6
Yin and Yang

OK, I promised I'd avoid using as much jargon as I could. I'm going to use the terms **yin** & **yang** because they're so practical, and I know you're heard them before. Basically, they apply to any two kinds of complimentary opposites. If *hot* is *yang*, then *cold* is *yin*. If *dry* is *yang*, then *wet* is *yin*. If *full* is *yang*, then *empty* is *yin*. Get it? Opposites, that's all.

Now, in my experience, all of meditation, regardless of style or culture, aims either at emptying the mind of input or focuses on narrowing the mind's awareness of a specific input. Both methods are good for achieving calmness, and focus. Each type is good for achieving different goals, and each appeals to different people. There are also a few potential pitfalls, not so much dangers but things to watch out for, associated with each.

YIN

When I talk about "yin" techniques in this book, I'll be referring to the kind of meditations where you seek to empty your mind, and keep it that way. Just for a little while, of course.

YANG

When I talk about "yang" techniques in this book, I'll be talking about the kind of techniques were you put something in your attention for your mind to focus on, like an image or a prayer or a mantra, or taking a specific action.

YIN TECHNIQUES

I bet when you first think about meditation, you imagine some Buddhist monk sitting in an incense-smoke clouded temple, with his mind blissfully free of any thought. Empty. "No Mind."

Now, why would you want to stop your mind? Most people don't realize how many thoughts are running through their mind every second of their waking day. It's a sort of a silent narration, and you may be only occasionally aware of it, but it really goes on all the time. Part of the function of this *internal narration* is to reinforce to the mind what's happening right now, so that it knows where it is all the time. It sort of provides a continual status update as to what's going on. And that's got to be a good thing, right? Well, yes and no. The information that this internal chatter runs is made up of observations, but also of feelings and opinions, and even bits of information it may have picked up in error, other people's opinions, bits of information from advertising, even stuff from songs and movies. Funny thing is that the more stressful your day is, the more these status updates run through the back of your mind, like an endless news-radio loop. What's worse, the information in these loops acts like a filter for the information that comes into you. If incoming information doesn't match what you're inner mind is hearing in these radio-loops, it just filters out the new info. Think about it. Did you ever have one of those days where the message in your mind kept reinforcing what a crappy Monday it is, and it just seems like everything that you're aware of is just as crappy, or worse? Maybe you're cursed, but maybe the curse is just that the negative info-loop in your head is filtering out the things that would otherwise turn your day around.

Sort of makes sense to try to just stop all this chatter for a while, at least long enough to be able to examine it, and maybe to write a better script for it.

It takes a knack to be able to keep your mind empty, since, as the saying goes, nature abhors a vacuum. Trying to just keep your mind empty is like developing a particular muscle in your mind, one that will hold back the river of thoughts. Like developing any muscle, some people can just start working that muscle, while others have to gradually build it up.

Once you have your mind empty, you can begin to become more aware of all the things you weren't aware of before. All the other things your senses are picking up, memories, feelings, thoughts. You may find that you're more aware of many things you took for granted. At the same time, once you clear out your mind, you might also become aware of what's *inside*: deeper thoughts and ideas lurking in the background that just never had a chance to compete with all of that other stuff. Maybe intuitions or inspirations.

Sweeping the thoughts out of your mind for a little while is a good way to get back in touch with who you are and what you're feeling. It can help you get a little perspective on issues on your life, help you get in touch with your own creativity and maybe even your intuition. It can even improve your health.

YANG TECHNIQUES

These are meditation techniques where you are doing something. Maybe visualizing a thing or a scene or even a story, listening to something, maybe even making a sound, or repeating a mantra or a prayer, or doing some other sort of activity. These active techniques give you a sort of mental tool or target to focus on. You can also use these kinds of techniques for putting new thoughts and ideas into your mental system. Some people even feel you can change the world around you a little bit, like people who pray for world peace. I hope they're right!

While you're focusing on these mental targets, whether an image or a prayer you're repeating, you increase your focus, and all the other thoughts will just kind of drop away. As with the yin techniques, you'll find a kind of peace by moving away from your daily thoughts for a little while.

Yin or Yang? What's right for you? I recommend starting with the first techniques in the book, since the later techniques build on the earlier ones. But if any technique really jumps out at you, try it! I've given you enough different things in this book that you WILL find some that work for you pretty fast. Once you're familiar with the feeling of the meditative state, you can explore it with some of the other techniques. One of the neat things is that even though they offer similar goals, each one can give you a little different perspective, and help in different areas.

Chapter 7
Getting started

WHAT DO I NEED TO GET STARTED?

Not much: a mind, a body to put it in, a place to practice where you won't be disturbed, and some time.

If you're just starting out, shoot for 5-10 minutes. That's plenty of time to begin to get some results. Don't push yourself, that kind of defeats the purpose of the exercise. If you want, and you're able to, you can extend the time.

Try to find some time when you won't be disturbed by anyone else, and it's even better if you can commit to it a little bit every day. A little bit every day will get better, faster results than longer sessions over an irregular schedule, but you will get some benefits from any practice you can get away with.

A quick word of warning: The first couple of times you practice, you may not get the kind of results you were expecting. You may even feel a little bit crummy. If you've been having a lot of negativity or stress in your life, you may find some residual uncomfortability rising up as it clears out of your psyche. Occasionally, a little irritability or a mild headache might accompany your first couple of tries, but these should go away quickly. You should be finding a feeling of balance, peace, and contentment when doing these techniques. If you keep getting headaches, undesirable emotional experiences, detachment from everyday life or hallucinations, like hearing or seeing things, STOP! Talk to a qualified expert, maybe a mental healthcare professional. All of these techniques have the goal of helping you to function better in your everyday life. They shouldn't be making it more complicated.

DO I NEED ANY OTHER EQUIPMENT?

Well, a **timer** or a **clock** might be helpful for you to keep track of time.

Some people, particularly those following religious traditions, keep time by using a string of beads. This is common in Christian, Hindu, Buddhist, and Moslem traditions. It's usually called a **rosary** or a **mala**, and used when a person is counting off a particular number of prayer or mantra repetitions. One bead is pulled through the fingers for every repetition. You can use it for that, or even for counting off the number of breaths you take. I find the Indian mala very convenient, since they come in several different sizes—they look like bracelets or necklaces—and each size has a different number of beads, but most will be a division of the number 108, a number that is considered to have auspicious qualities. Hence, you can get a 108 bead mala that's like a necklace, or a 54-bead mala (2 x 54 – 108), a 27-bead mala (4 x 27 = 108), or an 18-bead mala that's like a bracelet (6 x 18 = 108). If I'm in a hurry, I might only have time for an 18-bead meditation, other times, I might want to go for the whole 108.

There's actually one extra bead on the mala, by the way. It's called the guru bead, and it's there to let you know when you've gone all the way around. It's usually strung perpendicular to the others, or it has a tassel attached, so you can feel it without stopping to look. When you hit it, you know you've gone a full round, and you can either stop or continue, if you like. In that way you could do 108 breaths on an 18 bead mala in six cycles. (In the Hindu tradition, when you get to that extra bead you usually reverse direction rather than crossing it and continuing in the same direction).

You can also make your own by simply tying knots or beads on a length of string.

CLOTHING

Wear whatever is comfortable. You can have special meditation robes, but your street clothes work just as well. Just make sure to loosen your belt or tie, or anything else that's tight, particularly around your neck and torso. Take off your shoes if it makes you comfortable, too.

A JOURNAL

Some people find it very helpful to keep a little notebook of their experiences and experiments. It's always fun to look back on where you were when you started, and the notebook can be a reminder to keep up with your practice!

INCENSE

If you like it, and it sets a mood, use it! If you don't like it, you certainly don't need it. (I'll include a neat little incense meditation for the olfactory-inclined).

In traditional use, incense served several purposes. It sanctified the place you practice, which is to say, it created a certain mood and a boundary to the place and was believed to clear away negative influences while feeding and attracting good ones. And a good-smelling perfume would do that, wouldn't it?

The second thing it did was create an atmosphere that encouraged the practice. If you're used to smelling a certain smell in conjunction with a certain activity, that smell gets you right in the mood for that activity the next time you hear it. Smells are well-known emotional triggers—think of the smell your favorite food, or that particular smell of your favorite holiday. Does it make you feel an emotion? Does it bring up a memory? For many people it happens automatically.

In Asian cultures, Incense, in the form of sticks, also served to keep the time. An incense stick of average length burns for about a half an hour. Some Japanese and Chinese sticks (the ones without the bamboo cores) were made to burn fairly precisely, in fact. In China they even had what was known as an incense clock. The burning stick was laid on a wire grid, and every time the burning end passed another wire on the grid, 10 minutes had elapsed. Neat, huh?

You can use incense to keep the time if it suits you. If you have your eyes closed you can notice when the smell starts to dissipate after the stick is finished. If you decide to use incense, be aware that some are made with synthetic materials that can give you headaches, and some are very smoky. You may have to search a little bit to find the one that puts you in the best mood. Fortunately, incense is generally pretty inexpensive, so you can try different ones for very little cost. Consider starting with the more traditional Indian, Tibetan or Japanese types. Those are usually the most agreeable to start with. Very cheap types or very fruity ones, like banana and strawberry, are more likely to be made with irritating synthetics.

Generally, an average stick, about 8" long, burns for about half an hour. A cone about 10 minutes.

CANDLES

Candles are used similarly in some traditions, particularly Western ones. A four-inch-long candle that's about ½" thick burns about four hours. A small votive candle may go for six hours.

Candles have been used as a focus point for certain kinds of meditation. See *Trataka*, later in this book.

Scented candles may be good for creating a mood, like incense.

SEATING

There are even special meditation cushions to sit on. If you're not comfortable sitting on a chair or the floor, you can use a pillow or a folded-up blanket or towel.

DRUGS & SUBSTANCES

None of these will help your meditation experience. Caffeine will make it harder to relax. Alcohol, nicotine, sedatives, and other central nervous system depressants will make it harder for you to keep your focus. Same goes for psychedelics. Some people who use these drugs already find that meditation can lessen their dependency, or get rid of the need for these things entirely! You know, all of these chemicals are used, really, to help get a little better control over your mind. By the use of meditation we aim to get some control directly. Chemicals have side effects that may not be very healthy, and even when they do what they should, they wear off eventually, and have to be used again and again to get the desired results. Some are expensive. Some become less effective over time, while meditation practice improves over time. Wouldn't it be nice just to bypass the substances?

BASIC POSITIONS: STANDING, SITTING, LYING DOWN

There are a few standing meditations and we'll discuss those in the chapter on standing meditations.

Sitting: The most common way to meditate. In the western tradition you can sit on a chair. In much of the east they like to sit cross-legged on the floor, and this can be comfortable, particularly if you have a good pillow to sit on. Some Indian adepts like to sit in the "lotus" position, with the legs interlocked. It makes it easier to keep the upper body erect, but it takes special training to get the legs to interlock. In Japan, they like to sit in a way they call *seiza*, a sort of kneeling, with the shins on the floor and the torso centered over the ankles. It's good for keeping upright, but a little rough on the knees, particularly on hardwood floors.

Regardless which sitting position is right for you, they all have a few things in common. When you sit, you should be sitting up straight, so that your vertebrae are like a stack of poker chips, one on top of the other. Avoid leaning to one side or the other, since this will put stress on your back after a time, and make your sitting more uncomfortable. Some people say that you should sit as if there were a string tied to the very top of your head, and was pulling you up slightly, so that your torso and back just hung lightly over your hips. You may also find that sitting in this way makes it very easy to breathe. In this position some people find their head pulled back a little further than they're used to, but after a time they discover they're having a lot less stress on the back of their neck. You can explore in front of a mirror and see.

The nice thing about sitting is that no matter how deeply relaxed you get, sitting keeps you from falling asleep, which can happen when you lie down.

SITTING IN A CHAIR

This is a good way to start, and useful if you have knee or leg problems. Sit firmly on the chair, but a little forward of the back of it, so that your back isn't resting on the back of the chair, and your spine is erect, in the way we discussed in the last paragraph. Both feet should be flat on the floor, both legs spread slightly and comfortably, about the width of your hips. Your hands should rest on your knees, palm up or down or even on their edges, just as long as they're not going to slip off.

If you still have difficulty sitting up straight, it's OK to sit back on the chair, but still try to keep the spine as straight as you can.

CROSS-LEGGED SITTING

Best on the floor. This is a pretty common way to sit on the floor, but again, try to keep the spine as straight up and down as you can. The one problem with sitting this way is that it tends to curve the lower back out a bit, so sitting on a small cushion or pillow can be a help. You may fold your hands in your lap, or place them on your knees, either palm up or down, as illustrated below.

The reason the Yogis like that difficult-to-get-into "lotus position" that you might have seen before, is that the hips are aligned a little differently, and it makes it easy to keep the spine straight. I don't personally use the lotus position, so I'm not including it on the book, but you can find it in many books and websites about yoga, if you're curious.

JAPANESE SEIZA SITTING

Kneel, place your shins flat on the floor with the tops of your feet on the floor as well, and bring your body straight down until it rests lightly on the heels. As always, keep the spine straight and erect, head up and back. Allow the knees to spread a bit, "the width of one or two fists," and keep your feet together. After you're in this position a while, you might be tempted to slouch a bit, and let yourself "mush down." Try to avoid that.

LYING DOWN

In yoga, they call this the "corpse position": lying down with the back flat on the floor and the palms up. In this position you can relax every muscle. It's a very relaxing position, but it's not ideal for meditation, except for the advanced meditator, since it's very easy to drift off into sleep.

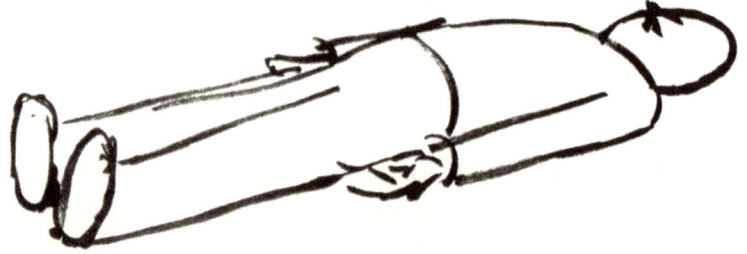

The sitting positions are very good for getting your mind to the *alpha level*, since they allow relaxation, but a certain level of awareness is still necessary, and that keeps you from going to sleep. Lying down in the "corpse position" allows you to drift into the deeper *theta level*—if you don't fall asleep!

BACK STRETCH

If you're not used to sitting in the ways I described, you may find the muscles of your back complaining the first few times. You can try a little stretching before and after, to loosen up the muscles. If the discomfort doesn't go away or it gets worse, see a doctor.

Bending forward in the toe-touching position is a good way to loosen up those lower back muscles. If you're not used to that stretch, try it like this: Stand up straight, raise your hands over your head and bend backwards a bit, then begin to bend forward slowly and let yourself go as far as you can while still staying totally relaxed. When you've gone as far as you comfortably can, just let the muscles relax as far as they're willing to by themselves. Inhale, exhale, relax, and

notice how much further you naturally stretch on the exhale, and then inhale again. When you've had enough, rise up slowly till you're standing. Repeat a few times. Then shake yourself out a little bit, and notice how you feel. Remember not to tense your muscles on the stretch, and just allow the weight of your body to stretch itself.

Practice in whatever way is convenient to you, but keep in mind that regular practice, even a little each day, will yield the fastest results.

OK, we're ready to begin!

First thing to do:

RELAX!

Chapter 8
Relax!

Relax!

Go on, just do it! Now!

I said relax!

Not so easy? OK, here's a great way to relax if you're so tense you just can't.

SIMPLE RELAXATION TECHNIQUE

When you're really feeling some kind of feeling strongly, you can't just turn it around. I mean, when you really feel angry or sad, and someone insists you cheer up, does it work? *Hey little clown, turn that frown upside-down!* That's really annoying, ain't it? When you're feeling strongly in a particular way, it's really hard to *just* do the opposite.

So, I say, don't! For example, if you're tense, *acknowledge that tension*, and you know what? You'll be able to relax more easily. Try the following. *Please read through all the steps before starting.* (FYI: It works even if you're not tense):

1) —Sit down. A chair is ideal for this but you should use whatever position you like best.

   —Take a deep breath, hold it for a second, and let it out.

—Raise one arm straight out in front of you, as if you're pointing at something across from you. Make a fist at the end of that arm.

—Here we go: Take a deep breath, and hold it! While you're holding it, tighten up every muscle in your arm. Clench that fist as tight as you can. I'm talking white knuckled, iron-bar rigid. HOLD it! Got it as tight as you can? Keep holding your breath and tighten it even more! Now hold it—and your breath—and in your mind count: one—two—three.

—On three, exhale hard and loud, and allow that arm to just drop, flop into your lap. Loose and limp as a wet old noodle. This is important: At **the same time, say "relax" either aloud or to yourself, and touch the tip of your thumb and your middle finger of the other hand**, like making an "OK" gesture. I'll explain it at the end of the exercise, but for now, trust me and do it.

—Feel that relaxation in your whole arm, and your shoulder.

2) Same drill, but this time we're going to do the legs, that's why sitting in a chair is ideal. Sitting cross-legged might give you cramps.

—Take a deep breath, hold it for a second, and let it out.

—Here we go: Take a deep breath, and hold it! While you're holding it, tighten up every muscle in your legs, both of them, as tight as you can. HOLD it! Got it as tight as you can? Keep holding your breath and tighten even more! Now hold it, and your breath, and in your mind count: one—two—three.

—On three, exhale hard and loud, and allow those legs to go just as relaxed as they can, as if they're like smoke blowing away on the wind. So loose and so very limp. **At the same time, say "relax" either aloud or to yourself, and touch the tip of your thumb to your middle finger.**

—Feel that relaxation in your whole lower body.

And if there are any places that still feel tight down there, use your mind to spread the relaxation.

3) Last time! This time we go for the whole body, both arms, legs, your head and your face. Ready?

—Take a deep breath, hold it for a second, and let it out.

—Here we go: Take a deep breath, and hold it! While you're holding it, tighten up every muscle in your legs, both of them, your arms, your belly, your chest, your neck, your head, even your face: scrooch up your mouth, eyes, nose, really tight. HOLD it! Got it as tight as you can? Keep holding your breath and tighten it even more! Now hold it, and your breath and in your mind count: one—two—three.

—On three, exhale hard and loud, and let everything go loose and floppy. Just slouch down, let your head loll, your lips loose & floppy, eyes relaxed, your hands dangling, your back totally relaxed, tummy loose. I mean, everything! **At the same time, say "relax" either aloud or to yourself, and touch the tip of your thumb to your middle finger.**

Feeling more relaxed?

The more you practice this, the less effort you'll need to just drop off all of that stress and relax when you want to.

In fact, with a little bit of practice, you'll find that all you have to do is say to yourself "relax" and touch your thumb tip to your middle finger and it'll remind your body of exactly that great feeling of relaxation. With practice, the OK gesture, touching your thumb-tip and middle finger together will become an "anchor" for the feeling. It becomes associated in your mind, and once it does, you can use it as an on-switch for that feeling of relaxation.

Chapter 9
Breathe!

A lot of tension is caused just by breathing too tightly. If your body can't draw air freely and easily, it will instinctively feel threatened, and stay tense. That's one way your breathing controls your physicality. Actors are trained to adjust their breathing to control the emotions they portray, and just by changing the way they breathe, they can change everything about their demeanor, from saints to villains. What is your breathing conveying about you?

Early in life you're told to stand straight and suck in your tummy, because it makes you look better and trimmer and breathe higher up in the chest. Know what? When you do this, you limit the amount of air your lungs can take in. When you breathe from high up in the chest, you're primarily using your ribs to breathe, and that only allows your lungs to fill about halfway. It's a funny thing, because as babies we breathe from our tummies, using a muscle called the *diaphragm*. It's a sheet of muscle across the bottom of the ribcage, and it can fill your lungs much more efficiently, especially when combined with a little upper chest breathing.

To understand the difference between the types of breathing, try this experiment:

Chest breathing—Stand in front of a mirror, if you have one handy. Its helpful, but not entirely necessary. Exhale, and put your hands on your tummy. As you exhale, suck that tummy all the way in. Now inhale using just your chest. Your chest will typically rise, and your shoulders will, too. Make sure your tummy stays

sucked in, though. Got it? OK, relax. This is pure chest breathing. Try it a few times if you're not sure. Even when you take a deep breath, you really don't draw in all that much air. What's more, did you notice that you probably felt a little tense when you inhaled? Certainly not very relaxed.

Pure upper-chest breathing, slightly exaggerated. The shoulders rise and upper ribcage expands.

Diaphragmatic (belly) breathing—Stand in front of a long mirror, if you have one handy. If not, you can do without. Exhale, and put your hands on your chest. Now inhale, but this time keep your chest down, and just let your tummy inflate, like a big Santa Claus. Don't force it, but rather, let it expand in all directions, like a beach ball inflating. Relax. What did you notice? Try it again a few times. The first thing most folks notice is that their shoulders and upper body doesn't get as tense as it does with chest breathing. A lot of people notice they can take in more air. Diaphragmatic breathing draws in more air for most people, but it's still not complete.

Pure abdominal breathing, slightly exaggerated. The shoulders stay down and belly expands.

BEST OF BOTH WORLDS

The kind of breathing I like is a **mixture of the two**. Try this now: Hands at your sides, facing a mirror if you're using one. Exhale. Start inhaling diaphragmatically. Inhale by expanding your belly, and when that's gone as far as it can *without forcing it*, continue the inhale by allowing your chest to inflate *just enough* to be comfortable. Try it a few times. As you get comfortable with it, you'll notice your breathing slows down. Because each breath takes in more air, you don't have to breathe as quickly. This alone helps most people to relax. Did you ever notice that under stress most people breathe faster? Slow down the breathing and you slow down the pace your body's running at, which can be a big help in staying calmer.

Spend some time practicing this way of breathing so that you can do it comfortably and naturally whenever you want to or need to.

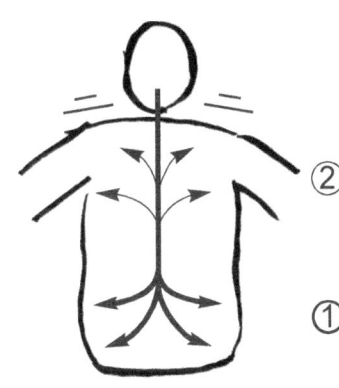

2. SECOND, when the belly has expanded as much as it can comfortably, continue the inhale allowing the chest to expand as much as it can comfortably, without raising the shoulders.

1. FIRST, draw the breath downwards into the belly area, an allow it to expand, without forcing it.

Chapter 10
The basic technique

MEDITATION 1—BREATHING

Time to get started meditating!

This will be a seated meditation. Partly yin and partly yang. I recommend getting comfortable doing this for at least a couple of weeks before going on to any of the others. In some traditions of meditation, this is all they need. This will give you a good foundation, and by itself it is a very powerful meditation, too. You should begin to feel calmer and more focused quickly.

1) Sit down in your preferred position. Be sure you're comfortable, you won't be disturbed for a few minutes, and your back is straight. You can close your eyes if you want.

2) Now, relax. If you want to, use the tense-and-relax method from **chapter 7**. Or just allow your body to unwind.

3) We're going to breathe for 10 breaths, using the combined breathing we talked about in the previous chapter. Ready?

4) Inhale, slowly, but naturally, diaphragm (belly) first, then chest. Hold it a moment. Exhale, just as slowly. Some people notice a pleasant quietness just at the moment between breathing in and breathing out. Did you? Be sure to make the in-breath and the out-breath take the same length of time.

5) Inhale, pause, exhale. Count. Repeat 9 more times.

How was that for you? How does your body feel? This is a very good meditation to start with. Just pay attention to your breathing and your sitting, and let everything else slide. By focusing on your breathing, you're naturally taking your attention away from all the other thoughts floating around in your head. Some people even like to focus on the *pause* between the breaths. Your circulation system will appreciate the slow, regular rhythm. After you've gotten comfortable with this kind of breathing, you won't tend to notice when you do it, *unless you want to*. You can always *choose* to pay attention to your breathing.

Don't focus on anything except your breath. When thoughts come into your mind, just let them go where they will. The only thing you have to do is pay attention to your breathing. Explore the best way to breathe to allow you to feel relaxed. Maybe even centered.

I'd recommend you do this one for a while before going on to other techniques. This one is a goodie, and is also the basis of many of the others. Try to do it at the same time every day for a week or more, and if you want to, you can journal your experiences.

I recommended 10 breaths for the very first time, which should only take a few minutes. But if you like, you can continue longer. Three to five minutes is very good, ten minutes is great! A little every day will yield great results.

Chapter 11
Meditations on the Yin side

I hope you've been using the techniques you've learned so far, and are getting good results from them. Here are some more. If you've been getting good results from the first meditation, and you're starting to understand the feeling of where you're going, then try the flavor of some of these, and see what they do for your results.

MEDITATION 2—EMPTYING YOUR MIND OF SOUNDS AND WORDS

1) Assume your favorite sitting position. Be sure you're comfortable, you won't be disturbed for a few minutes, and your back is straight.

2) Close your eyes.

3) Now, relax. If you want to, use the tense-and-relax method from **chapter 7**. Or just allow your body to unwind.

4) Breathe in the way we practiced—slowly and deeply. Do this for a few moments until everything about you is calm and still.

5) Turn your attention to the sounds inside your mind, and tune out any sounds outside of you. Remember that if there's an emergency, you will still always be able to respond instantly.

6) Pay special attention to your internal dialogue, and any sounds or thoughts that come through your imagination. Just be aware of them, without reacting to them in any way. Spend a little while this way, until you're familiar with them, maybe a few minutes or whatever feels right for you.

7) Now, think of stillness and silence. Quiet your inner mind and experience a warm, peaceful, relaxing, secure silence. Some people think of the quiet in a church or temple, or a museum, or even the comfy quiet under the covers of your bed.

8) If it helps, imagine a little particle of this peaceful stillness in the middle of your head, and imagine it expanding gently outwards in all directions to ease the sounds out. Alternatively, you can just imagine silence, the internal noises gradually fading downwards.

9) When you achieve the silence, hold it, and enjoy the peaceful stillness.

10) During the stillness, thoughts may begin to come up into your awareness. Just hold onto the stillness and let the thoughts go. Eventually, the stillness will strengthen, like a muscle.

11) When you're ready to finish, become aware of the sounds around you. Open your eyes. Give yourself a few minutes to come back up to full waking speed.

How was that for you? If it was easy, you're doing very well! Most people find this very, very hard! Some people spend years trying to perfect this. Nature abhors a vacuum, and that includes making your mind a vacuum. Some days it almost seems like when you do this you just suck thoughts into your head. But don't give up. It's really no different from strengthening a muscle, regular practice cannot fail to produce results.

This is a kind of yin meditation. You're not actively exercising anything but stillness.

What is this kind of meditation good for?

It's very peaceful. It can be very calming and restorative, particularly for people who work with ideas a lot, or with other people, or lots of noises. With practice, it's like a quiet garden you can retreat to, inside you. What's more, when you can hold the silence for a little while, you can have a little more control over the sounds and thoughts you let in. And by stilling the thoughts inside your head for a short time, including the ones your mind generates seemingly at random, you sometimes make room for fresh thoughts and insights.

Some people even find that after doing this for a while, they begin to be aware of things in their life that they had taken for granted, and knowing them in a new way.

MEDITATION 3—EMPTYING YOUR MIND OF IMAGERY

1) Assume your favorite sitting position. Be sure you're comfortable, that you won't be disturbed for a few minutes, and your back is straight.

2) Close your eyes.

3) Now, relax. If you want to, use the tense-and-relax method from **chapter 7**. Or just allow your body to unwind.

4) Breathe in the way we practiced—slowly and deeply. Do this for a few moments until everything about you is calm and still.

5) Turn your attention inwards, and tune out any sounds outside of you. Remember that if there's an emergency, you will still always be able to respond instantly.

6) Pay special attention to your internal imagery, and any pictures, shapes or colors that come through your imagination. Just be aware of them, without reacting to them in any way. Spend a little while this way, until you're familiar with them, maybe a few minutes, or whatever feels right for you.

7) Think of stillness and emptiness. A dark, peaceful, secure emptiness. Some people think of a movie screen that's gone dark, right after the end of a really great movie, or the sky at night, with no moon or stars, just endless openness and possibility, or a room with no lights, no walls or ceiling or floor, just endless, limitless possibilities.

8) Expand it outwards, so you have all the space you could ever need.

9) Hold the emptiness, enjoy the peaceful stillness.

10) During the stillness, images may begin to come up into your awareness. Just hold onto the stillness and let those thoughts go. Eventually, the stillness will strengthen, like a muscle.

11) When you're ready to finish, open your eyes, and be aware of the colors and shapes of the things around you. Give yourself a few minutes to come back up to full waking speed.

How was that for you? You'll notice it was virtually the same as the previous meditation, however it's addressing the *visual* instead of the *auditory*. The benefits and effects of this meditation are very similar to the last one. Obviously, it's good for someone who uses their eyes a lot.

Internally, the unconscious often codes thoughts and feelings in *visual metaphors*. These are pictures that represent complicated thoughts. Did you ever notice that sometimes, when you close your eyes, maybe just before you're going to sleep, or when you're just resting your eyes, pictures just kind of pop into your head? Some of these are memories, or things you were thinking about during the day, but sometimes you see pictures and you have no idea where they came from. Those are often metaphoric images believed to be produced as your inner mind goes through its daily processes, similar to the internal dialogue. This meditation can help clear out some of the old thought processes, and let you start afresh.

MEDITATION 4: CLEARING YOUR MIND OF BODILY SENSATIONS

1) Assume your favorite sitting position. Be sure you're comfortable, you won't be disturbed for a few minutes, and your back is straight.

2) Close your eyes.

3) Now, relax. If you want to, use the tense-and-relax method from **chapter 7**. Or just allow your body to unwind.

4) Breathe in the way we practiced—slowly and deeply. Do this for a few moments until everything about you is calm and still.

5) Turn your attention inwards, and tune out any sensations outside of you. Remember that if there's an emergency, you will still always be able to respond instantly.

6) Pay special attention to your body. What are you feeling? What is your body telling you? If you are relaxed and comfortable in your sitting and breathing, you shouldn't have many strong sensations, but you'll still be feeling something. Just allow yourself to feel whatever you're feeling.

7) Think of stillness and solidness as if your body were as still as a mountain, or a tree in a quiet forest, a forest without wind or movement of any kind. Just quiet peace. Still and solid.

8) Expand the feeling of stillness in your body.

9) Hold the peaceful stillness.

10) During that stillness, sensations or thoughts may begin to come up into your awareness. Just hold onto the stillness and let those sensations go. Eventually, the stillness will strengthen, like a muscle.

11) When you're ready to finish, open your eyes, and be aware of the feelings within you and around you. Give yourself a few minutes to come back up to full waking speed.

This is another variation of the previous yin meditation for emptying your mind. These aren't easy! Of course you probably know that by now. They strengthen your ability to focus and concentrate. They can help you to learn about yourself and how much power you really have over yourself, and they can really help clear out all those cobwebs from your awareness.

After you practice these for a while, you may begin to come up with your own variations. Find what works best for you.

All of these practices make a great foundation for the yang meditations to follow.

Chapter 12
Meditations on the Yang side

Meditation is a funny thing. To a great extent, it's all about going inside yourself, getting in touch with the parts of yourself that you take for granted, maybe stripping off the stuff that the outside world layers on you, so that you can find the "real" you. But sometimes, it isn't easy to go inside. Your mind just won't go, or it does, but you get sleepy.

If your mind is really intent on not focusing on the inside, you can focus just as easily on something outside yourself, and use it to open the door to go in. Meditations where you focus outside yourself can feel very different energetically. While the ones that turn you completely inward are inherently relaxing, the ones that focus outward can be very energizing!

Some of these techniques utilize a little bit of equipment. I'll suggest the most common items, but feel free to improvise.

MEDITATION 5—FOCUS ON AN EXTERNAL SOUND

This is another way to clear your mind through your auditory senses, like **Meditation 2**, but this time, we use an actual sound to do it.

Traditionally, this technique is done with a single chime, a bell, or a gong. The instrument is struck once, and the meditator focuses on the diminishing sound. As the sound fades away, it takes more & more focus to hold onto the fading sound in your mind. By the time the sound is no longer audible, the meditator has finely tuned his focus on the sound left behind by the sound when it's gone. Kinda Zen, huh?

If you don't have a bell or a chime, you can pluck the string of a stringed instrument, like a guitar or a violin, or you can strike a single key on a piano. However, the simplest piece of equipment is a tall, everyday drinking glass, the kind you might serve iced tea in. Just tap it with the edge of a fork or a spoon (lightly!). That will give you the sound you need. You can even "tune" this chime by putting a little bit of water in it. The more water, the higher the pitch. And while we're at it, tapping it with a wooden spoon or a pencil will give a somewhat mellower sound.

I'm guessing you have the idea of this already, but here are the steps, one by one:

1) Prepare the device that you're going to use to sound your note. It should be in easy reach when you're sitting.

2) Assume your favorite sitting position and get comfortable and relaxed.

3) Control your breathing until it comes naturally, and you don't have to think about it.

4) Ready? Sound your chime, just once.

5) Close your eyes and focus on the sound. It'll be strong at first, then fade.

6) Put all your attention into following the sound with your hearing for as long as you can.

7) When you're sure you can't hear it any more, listen to what's left behind. This is the main body of the meditation.

8) If you find your attention waning, strike your instrument again, and repeat the process.

9) When you're ready to finish, open your eyes, and be aware of the feelings within you and around you. Give yourself a few minutes to come back up to full waking speed.

The sound provides a very nice way to get into the right focus. Some people find that their hearing acuity actually seems to improve with this exercise.

HERE'S A SECOND VARIATION:

Instead of focusing on a sound from an external instrument, we're going to vocalize a simple sound, a simple *mantra*. I'm going to suggest the Indian word Om. It's pronounced with a long "o" as if you're saying "**Oh m**y goodness!" If you prefer, you can use any vowel sound ("Aaaah," "Eeeeh," "Iiiiih," "Ooooh," or even "Uuuuh.").

The character for "om."

When you make the sound, imagine it coming up from the bottom of your torso, and rising up through your body all the way up to the top of your head. Don't rush it, imagine really feeling it move up inside you. Some people can do a single "Om" lasting 30 seconds. That takes some breath strength! Practice it a few times before you try it in meditation. Try to maintain your breath strength from beginning to end. As you reach the end, just allow the sound to fade out. Imagine that it's still going even after you're not making a sound anymore.

Here's the meditation:

1) Assume your favorite sitting position, and get comfortable and relaxed.

2) Control your breathing until it comes naturally, and you don't have to think about it.

3) Ready? Close your eyes and sound your "Om," just once.

4) Focus on the sound. It'll be strong at first, then fade.

5) Put all your attention into following the sound with your hearing for as long as you can, even while making the sound.

6) When you're sure you can't hear it any more, listen to what's left behind. This is the main body of the meditation.

7) If you find your attention waning, sound the "Om" again, and repeat the process.

8) When you're ready to finish, open your eyes, and be aware of the feelings within you and around you. Give yourself a few minutes to come back up to full waking speed.

Kinda different, isn't it? For one thing, you'll notice the vibration in your head and body. This can be very otherworldly, and some people really like it, others don't.

Once you get used to this, you can try to substitute other sounds or single-syllable words that might be meaningful to you. The Theosophists of the early 20th century liked to use "I", as in "I am" to help them get a feeling of centeredness. Try "I am" for a while and see what it does for you.

MEDITATION 6—FOCUS ON AN EXTERNAL SIGHT

In the Indian tradition, focusing your sight on something like a target for purposes of meditation is called "Trataka." In addition to being very calming, and helping you develop a strong mental focus, it also helps you develop a strong, confident gaze.

I first started practicing this after a bad eye infection that temporarily damaged my sight in one eye. At the time, I was also in a very stressful job situation, and I credit this exercise with helping me stay energized and focused while stuck in a very bad place. It was also surprisingly relaxing! I think this may be my favorite meditation these days.

Since we'll be using our sight for this, we'll need something to look at. Here are a couple of good choices. The easiest is just to sit a few feet away from a wall, and look for any kind of a mark on the wall that's at eye level when you're sitting. If there isn't any noticeable spot, all you need is a little dot. The traditional "target" for Trataka looks like this:

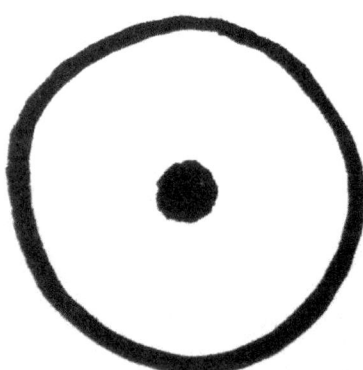

You can draw a circle about an inch or more in diameter and put a small dot in the middle. Black ink on white paper is easiest to see. You can put it on the wall at eye level with double stick tape.

Another option that works well for a "target" is the light on the tip of a stick of burning incense. Place it in a suitable incense burner, on a table at about eye level. Make sure there's nothing flammable around it—no loose papers, curtains, books, and so forth. Never leave it unattended!

Candles are also used both by Indian trataka practitioners and by Western mystical enthusiasts. Generally a tall thin taper is preferred. The flame of a thick pillar or votive candle becomes hard to see when it burns down into the candle. If you choose to use a candle, fix your gaze at the blue part at the base of the wick. I'm not sure whether it's a good thing for your eyes to stare into a flame for extended periods of time, so practice cautiously and sensibly. Don't hurt your eyes.

One more thing. There's a tricky part to this meditation: Don't Blink! Really—it's not easy. You probably won't be able to do it for long at first, but you will with time, and you'll develop a strong, confident gaze, too.

Whatever you use, the procedure is pretty much the same:

1) Assume your favorite sitting position, facing your target (the dot on the wall, your stick of incense, etc). Get comfortable and relaxed.

2) Control your breathing until it comes naturally, and you don't have to think about it.

3) Fix your eyes on the target.

4) Put all your attention into watching without blinking.

5) Just notice whatever you notice. Ignore any thoughts that might sneak through your mind.

8) When you're ready to finish, be aware of the feelings within you and around you. Give yourself a few minutes to come back up to full waking speed.

Try it for, say, 3-5 minutes the first time. Remember, most sticks of incense burn for about half an hour. Think you can go that long?

At first, your eyes will probably water quite a bit, that's OK. After a while this exercise will become fun & easy!

MEDITATION 7—FOCUS ON A PHYSICAL FEELING

This kind of meditation is good when you're already feeling pretty centered and solid, and you want to explore the boundaries between yourself and everything else.

What kind of physical feelings can you focus on? Think about these and try one you like:

The air on your skin

The lingering taste of a bite of food or a sip of tea (or wine, as you like...)

The feeling of your body as you sit

The feeling of your breath as it goes in and out

The feeling of your heart & blood moving

Any feeling that is significant to you!

1) Assume your favorite sitting position. Get comfortable and relaxed.

2) Control your breathing until it comes naturally, and you don't have to think about it.

3) Ready? Turn your attention to the sensation of your choice.

4) Close your eyes and focus on the chosen feeling. Really study that sensation. What do you notice? Texture, color, shape, sound, volume, temperature? What new things can you learn from it?

5) Continue for your specified time.

6) When you're done, open your eyes, and take a deep breath. Touch something to ground yourself—the floor or your sleeve or whatever is convenient.

A practice like this can help you get in touch with physical subtleties that you may not have been aware of before. If you're already intimate with a certain sensation, for example, if you're a chef who has to have a keen sense of taste, this sort of practice can let you use what you already have to achieve more calmness & relaxation, and maybe even open up new depths to your senses.

MEDITATION 8—FOCUS ON AN EXTERNAL SMELL

You're going to need something that generates an inspiring smell:

A bunch of fresh flowers

A green field, or a beach (or any fragrant, quiet location)

A scented candle, potpourri, or incense

Herbs or fruits

Perfume

Perhaps a food with a significant smell: Fresh-baked cookies, the scent of tea, or a bowl of chicken soup

I think you can guess the way this goes, but notice that I've added a little twist, so read through all the steps carefully, then place yourself where you can enjoy the smell, and let it lead you away…

1) Assume your favorite sitting position. Get comfortable and relaxed.

2) Control your breathing until it comes naturally, and you don't have to think about it.

3) Ready? Turn your attention to the aroma of your choice.

4) Close your eyes and focus on the scent. Really study it. What thoughts does it bring to mind?

5) Let those thoughts go after a while. What feelings does it bring to mind?

6) Let those feelings go. Then let yourself go, too…

7) When you feel you've accomplished something, a feeling of a new learning, or when it just feels right, it's time to conclude.

8) Open your eyes, and take a deep breath.

Many people find that smell is more connected to memories than other physical sensations.

> You know, I often think back to an afternoon I spent alone, lying on a beach in Barbados. The sun was bright overhead, the sand, fine and white under me. To my left, a line of dark green palm trees stretched on as far as I could see, and to my right the rhythmic rush of little waves from a brilliant blue ocean rang in my ear. I spent all afternoon on that beach. The clean ocean air revitalized my every breath, and what pulled it all together was a scent, like perfume, blowing in from someplace miles down the beach. Somebody must have been burning a fruitwood

> tree, maybe a flowering frangipani or some kind of wood I'd never smelled before, and the perfect, natural, incense-like smell, sweet and woody, traveled down the beach on the pleasant breeze for miles, and lingered on, over the sand where I sat...

SECTION B—FOCUS ON INTERNAL SENSATION

Here's a funny thing: did you ever have a song running through your head, and you couldn't shake it? Maybe you saw a scene or a face, and it just kept popping back in your mind's eye?

This is an effect we can use as a meditation tool, in a controlled way.

In the next section, I'm going to offer you some meditations that are similar to the ones in the previous section, but instead of using outside stimulus, you're going to something you create inside yourself. This kind of meditation is excellent for controlling your own thoughts and your will power—if you can do it!

These also make an excellent continuation of the previous exercises.

MEDITATION 9—FOCUS ON AN INTERNAL SOUND

That song in your head you can't shake, or the voice of a loved one, or a teacher that still rings in your head years after that voice spoke. These things seem almost real, and yet you know they're not. In the 80s, disco songs with simple lyrics and strong, rhythmic beats tormented disco lovers and haters alike by taking residence in our heads and banging on and on for hours after we'd heard them. If one of those bits of music popped into your head in the morning, you could be sure that it would be with you all day, each time digging a little deeper, like a cart's wheels going over the same tracks in the soft earth.

With that in mind, why not use this effect *deliberately*, in a good way, for your own advancement?

 Let's practice with the same sound that we used earlier in **Meditation 5—Om**. (If you aren't familiar with **Meditation 5**, you may want to go back to it first).

Meditating on an internal sound:

1) Assume your favorite sitting position, and get comfortable and relaxed.

2) Control your breathing, until it comes naturally, and you don't have to think about it.

3) Ready? Sound your "Om" the way you did before.

4) Close your eyes and focus on the sound. Strong at first, then let it fade. Try to record the sound in your head, as if your mind were a tape-recorder.

5) Put all your attention into replaying the sound inside your mind, but don't make any sound out loud! Replay it in your mind, only, and hear it for as long as you can, as you allow it to gradually fade.

6) When you're sure you can't hear it any more, listen to what's left behind.

7) If you find your attention waning, sound the "om" again, and repeat the process.

8) When you feel you're done, get up and move about. You may want to sing a little bit or talk to a friend, or get up and go outside, so that the sound doesn't keep playing in your mind. You'll find that you can get control over it pretty quickly, but the first few times, it may want to stick with you longer than you want it to.

Some people find that when they've done this for a while, their auditory acuity increases. They become more sensitive to sound and are aware of more of what their hearing, and they can recall more of what they hear. See what it does for you.

> Thirty years ago, when I was a teenager, I started taking fencing lessons from a mad old German fencing master in my neighborhood (in 1970s New York, you could still find mad old German masters in your neighborhood). He was blind in one eye, and had a shock of white hair, huge shoes, and despite looking like he was about 130 years old, he could move like lightning, and, with a sword in his hand, he never missed. He taught a very old style of fencing, one that included a system of "yells,'"something like the "kiai" that a Karate practitioner yells, but a little bit more involved. A technique might have three or four parts, and all had to be executed in a particular order, with a particular force, and all within a fraction of a second, and each bit had its own particular yell. So, as he demonstrated it to us, he shouted as he lunged and thrusted: "ooo—EH—LA!" Later on, I fenced in college, and competed for about ten years after, even taught a little bit, and still pick up a sword

> occasionally. And every time I do, even thirty years later, when I do that particular technique, I can still hear that trumpet-voice of his call "ooo—EH—LA!" And if I follow it exactly, I never miss.

MEDITATION 10—FOCUS ON AN INTERNAL SIGHT (VISUALIZATION)

If you're familiar with the current self-help materials in print and on the Internet, you know that, right now, "visualization" is all the rage. People talk about the power of visualizing your goals, visualizing your ideal physical state, visualizing yourself in your ideal place. You'll find tons of talk about the usefulness of meditation with visualization for changing yourself, and even changing your fortunes and your future.

Some people are naturally very visual, and can construct beautiful and complicated pictures and diagrams in their head. If you're one of those, you'll probably really like this exercise.

If you're reading this right now and saying: "I HATE this! I CAN'T visualize!" then you may want to explore this meditation a little more carefully, and I'm directing the next few paragraphs specifically to you.

OK, you tell me you're *sure* you can't visualize. Well, it's possible that's true. But first, let's try this experiment and see what happens: when you got up today, you got up and walked into another room (unless you're still in bed). Which room was it? Bathroom? Kitchen? Remember which room you went into. What color are the walls? What kind of furniture was in there? Was there a window? What shape was it? What color? If you can answer these questions—surprise!—you're visualizing! That's really all there is to it. Maybe you *believed* there was more to visualization?

> People sometimes get hung up on the *word* "visualize" and what it's supposed to mean. Now, one of the things that meditation's *supposed* to help you do, is cut through to the real meanings of things. "Visualize" just means to imagine visually. Never get hung up on any kind of "supposed to" for anything. That's just another limiting belief. Do things the way that's right for you, not the way someone else tells you you're supposed to do anything. Who says they're right, anyway?

I'm going to offer you a few variations of this meditation. Try the one you like the best, or try them all.

VARIATION A—A PICTURE

Find a picture of a single, simple object that appeals to you. A picture of a fruit, a flower, an animal, or even a book. Don't use a picture of a face or a person (yet) since it's too complicated. Keep it simple. Have that picture within easy reach when you first start.

1) Assume your favorite sitting posture. Get comfortable and relaxed. Have your picture handy.

2) Control your breathing until it comes naturally, and you don't have to think about it.

3) Look at your picture. Notice everything you can about it. Color, shape, texture, size. Notice the space around it that's not it. Really spend a lot of time studying it, until you've seen everything you can possibly see about it. When you're sure there's nothing more to learn about it, shut your eyes.

4) Put all your attention into imagining that you can see that thing in your mind's eye. Notice all the details you noticed when you were looking at your picture. If they aren't there, put them in with your mind's eye.

5) Now, hold that image in your mind for as long as you can. It may not be easy. It may want to fight, to wiggle, change shape or color. Be strong. Be in control.

6) When you begin to get a good picture in your mind, you may find that questions arise. Is there something else that should be in that picture, but you can't remember what it is? Is the color off, just a little bit? Good! Really try to remember as best you can, and try some more. You'll probably get it. If you're stumped, take a peek at your picture, and go right back to your mental image. Put in that missing detail.

7) When you're sure you've got the whole thing, hold it for as long as you can.

8) When you can't hold it any more, you can look at the picture, and start again.

9) When you feel it's time to stop, end the meditation. Look at the picture one more time and see if there was anything you missed.

Look around at some different things, to center yourself back in the here and now and clear your head.

Some people find that this strengthens their visual acuity. They begin to see more detail, and remember better. For some, it takes a while to get results, so give it time.

VARIATION B—COLORS

We're just going to focus on colors this time. I once read that people only dream in black and white, but I'm pretty sure I dream in color. What about you?

We'll start with three colors, but you can use as many as you want. The first few times, make a list of the colors in advance, but you can move more smoothly from one to the other.

So, let's start with the colors red, yellow, and green.

Think of a shade of red you really like. If it doesn't come to you easily, think of something that has that color—a rose, a clown's nose, a sunset.

Now think of a shade of yellow—like a flower, a sunrise, a yellow cupcake.

Finally, green—a field of grass, spinach, or a piece of green glass.

Got it? Let's go!

1) Assume your favorite sitting posture. Get comfortable and relaxed. Know your colors.

2) Control your breathing until it comes naturally, and you don't have to think about it.

3) Close your eyes, and take a few breaths while you look into the dark behind your closed eyelids. Colors or imagery may swim by. Just let them go. After a little while it'll stabilize. Imagine you're looking at a dark, picture-less movie screen.

4) Now, imagine someone just turned on a movie projector. The screen lights up with your first color—RED.

5) Now, **hold** that color in your mind for as long as you can. Be strong. Try to hold the color, bright and strong, for 10 slow breaths.

6) Now change to your second color—YELLOW. Hold for 10 breaths.

7) Now change to your third color—GREEN. Hold for 10 breaths. Is that green still strong after 10 slow breaths?

8) End by opening your eyes and looking around at some different things, to center yourself back in the here and now and clear your head.

You can do this with any colors you like, and you can increase the number of colors, or the length of time, or both. This meditation may increase your awareness of different colors. For example, how many different shades of red are you aware of?

VARIATION C—PICTURE AND COLOR COMBINED

We're going to combine the above two meditations. It's best if you've practiced both of those first until you're comfortable with them, before you start this one.

You're going to bring up the image that you visualized in **Variation A**. You'll have to be able to hold it for a moderately long time, so be sure you have that "mental photo." When you've got it stablized in your mind, you're going to change its color three times, like **Variation B**. This will give you a lot of control over your mind's eye. And just for fun, we're going to stretch that image too!

1) Assume your favorite sitting posture. Get comfortable and relaxed. Have your picture handy, and look at it to get a clear image in your head.

2) Control your breathing until it comes naturally, and you don't have to think about it.

3) Bring up that picture in your mind's eye, and if you have to, look at the picture first, to get the mental image and all its details. Hold it.

4) Notice all the details. Notice the colors and shapes.

5) Now, turn that object RED. Make the color strong and bright! See every detail of that object.

6) Hold that image for 10 slow breaths.

7) Now, turn that object YELLOW. Make the color strong and bright! See every detail of that object.

8) Hold that image for 10 slow breaths.

9) Now, turn that object GREEN. Make the color strong and bright! See every detail of that object.

10) Hold that image for 10 slow breaths.

11) Now pick the color you liked best and change the object to that color. If you're not sure which you liked best, go back to RED.

12) Stretch the object in your mind's eye, as it if were a rubber band. Stretch it twice as long, three times as long. Hold that image for 10 breaths. Notice every little detail.

13) Restore the image to its original shape and notice the differences.

14) When it's time to finish, open your eyes & look around. Clear the image from your mind.

With practice, this meditation can give you more control over your ability to visualize and construct things in your head. One of the attributes that "visual" people are supposed to have is the ability to "see things from all sides." This sexercise, with practice, can help you imagine things in alternate ways. "See" where it takes you.

MEDITATION 11—FOCUS ON AN INTERNAL FEELING

The feeling of happiness

The feeling of contentment

The feeling of joy

Any inner feeling that is significant to you or that you'd like to explore more

Now this one will take a little mental preparation. You're going to use a feeling as the tool for your exploration of sensation and inner calm, so prepare your tool in advance.

Pick a feeling, one of the above or your own. Take a minute to really explore what it means to you. What does it feel like—I mean, physically? Does it occupy a place in space or in relation to your body? Or in your body? Is there a color, a texture, a temperature? What does it mean to have this, or to need it? What does it make you think of? Why does it appeal to you? What are the questions you should ask that aren't listed here? Get to know it. Got it? You can even write it on a card or a piece of paper and put it in front of you before you begin. When you have it, we can begin.

1) Assume your favorite sitting position. Get comfortable and relaxed.

2) Control your breathing until it comes naturally, and you don't have to think about it.

3) Ready? Turn your attention to the feeling of your choice.

4) Close your eyes and focus on the feeling. Really study that sensation. Where is it in space? How does your body relate to it? What about it: Texture, color, shape, sound volume, temperature? What new learning can you get from it? Allow yourself time to really explore & experience everything you can.

5) When you feel you've accomplished something, a feeling of a new learning, or when it just feels right, it's time to conclude.

6) Open your eyes, and take a deep breath.

This meditation is a good way to alter your feelings or your outlook. I'm not saying much more about it, but don't sell it short. This is a very powerful technique for learning more about yourself.

We'll explore some more specific meditations for personal change in the next chapter.

Chapter 13
Active meditations for awareness and change

By now, we know that meditation is great way to calm the mind and get centered, to disentangle yourself from all the noise, fluff, and static of the everyday world all around us. If you've been practicing some of these techniques, you may be discovering an inner calm, or a better understanding of yourself, separate from your surroundings. Maybe getting a little more familiar with the inner you. Maybe even learning something about things that you've taken for granted before. If nothing more, you ought to be feeling a little bit calmer and more collected.

Did you know meditation can also be used for personal change? The following techniques can and have been used for a long, long time to achieve deeper states of meditation and also for self-development. See what they can do for you.

MEDITATION 12—FOCUS ON AN AFFIRMATION, MANTRA, OR PRAYER

> Here's a story from my days as a competitive fencer. First let me explain that fencing is a solitary sport. Each fencer is a team of one. So we'd usually show up at the competitions by ourselves, change into our uniforms and find a corner of the competition floor to organize our equipment and get ready. Fencing is scored electrically, and in order to do so, we had to have special wires worn inside our uniforms connected

to the swords. There were also grounding clips, connectors, and circuit-testers to be considered, along with the necessary sneakers, gloves, helmets, and weapons, and of course tools and tape for the inevitable last-minute repairs. Imagine a gym full of trained athletes, and every one mired in middle of their own private tangle.

Anyway, there was this one guy, a young kid, and I used to see him going through the same morning ordeal as the rest of us, and while he was doing it, his lips were moving to himself. I didn't know what he was saying, but I guessed it might be a song running through his head.

I noticed him fencing, though. He didn't seem to have been doing it long, but when he attacked he did so with enormous intensity, far more than one would expect for someone as inexperienced as he was.

Then I finally had the chance to fence with him. He made a lot of beginner's mistakes, but his intensity was unmistakable. He was TOUGH! During one particularly complicated exchange of attacks I got close enough to him to hear the words he was saying to himself: "I AM HERCULES! I AM HERCULES! I AM..." I think it worked for him.

The things you say to yourself, consciously or not, affect the way you see yourself and the way you see your world. A lot of people's lives are limited or freed by the words that run through their heads and the thoughts they think about themselves and their environment. And it's not just in the individual—it can be anyone or anything. So many slums and lost-cause neighborhoods have been reclaimed and rebuilt by people who saw the potential there instead of the limits.

Some people even believe that you can change your surroundings, your future, and your luck by the thoughts you hold.

At the very least, the way you feel is determined by the thoughts you hold, and it's proven that your health is affected by your feelings. So are other people around you that you communicate with, so who knows where it might end? Sounds like some experiments are in order....

Nearly one hundred years ago, a man named Emile Coué, a pharmacist and hypnosis pioneer, began to notice that many of his patient's ailments seemed to coincide with their mental state. The science of mind was very young then, but he wondered how much of his clients' ailments were being affected by their mind, so he tried a little experiment. He had one of his patients repeat a little phrase to themselves at every spare moment. The man began to feel better. Then he began to *get* better! He tried it with a few other patients and got very good results. After more experiments, he gave the world an affirmation that is still used successfully by many people:

"Every day, in every way, I'm getting better and better."

It was new to science, but it's not really a new idea. Various religions have been using prayers and mantras for personal change, and to create particular emotional states and get insights for centuries.

For example:

Ancient Christians travelling in foreign lands traditionally chanted this prayer for a feeling of strength and safety:

Kyrie Elieson which means "Lord have mercy."

Hindus, for thousands of years, have chanted mantras to recieve the blessings of various deities, develop spiritual powers, and protect them from bad luck. The Hindus have thousands of different mantras for every conceivable purpose, and swear by their efficacy. A common mantra to invoke Shiva, one of the major deities, for good luck and enlightenment is:

Om namo Shivaya, which means "praise and salutations to Shiva."

Buddhists also use mantras, and are famous for their popular mantra for enlightenment :

Om Mani Padmi Hum Which loosely translates into "the jewel in the lotus" but refers to the creative power of higher consciousness.

Theosophists of the early 20th century were the New Age movement of their time, which was called the "New Thought Movement." It strove to combine a rational, Western approach to the wave of Eastern philosophy that was making its way to the West, thanks to the industrial age's improved travel and communication. Theosophists were very interested in self-discovery, and often used to meditate simply by repeating or concentrating on *"I am."*

For the following exercises, pick a simple mantra or prayer to begin with, no more than a few words. You can try one of the above mentioned suggestions, or you can pick one of your own. You can even choose the first word that pops into your mind if you want to. There are several different ways you can use a prayer or a mantra.

VARIATION A—MEDITATING BY REPETITION

(For this one you may wish to use a string of prayer beads or a timer. Decide in advance how many repetitions you plan to do.) Some Indian sources suggest that there are three ways to recite—1) *Out loud*, which puts a lot of energy into your chanting; 2) *Softly, to yourself*, which is more practical when other people are around; 3) *Silently, to yourself*, which some sources think is the most powerful, since it requires more concentration to keep your mind from wandering. Try each a few times, and see how they feel to you:

1) Assume your favorite sitting position and get comfortable and relaxed. Close your eyes.

2) Control your breathing until it comes naturally, and you don't have to think about it.

3) Ready? Repeat your mantra a few times to warm up. Don't rush, pronounce it clearly. Find the natural rhythm of the words.

4) After a few practice repetitions, begin in earnest to repeat the mantra for the chosen number of repetitions. Continue at a measured pace. DON'T LET YOUR MIND WANDER!!

5) Put all your attention into the words you're repeating. Be aware of the sound of your words, how they make you feel, and what they mean to you. As you keep repeating, your feeling for the words may change. Allow the repetitions to occupy your full attention.

6) Be aware of your feelings and the sounds of the words.

7) When you're done, notice how you feel. One of the interesting things about this kind of meditation is that it quiets the mind by literally occupying it so your internal dialogue can't run. If you're repeating a positive message, your mind has no choice but to listen.

VARIATION B—CASUAL REPETITION

This is particularly useful with affirmations. You simply repeat your affirmation or mantra continually at every spare moment, while waiting for a train, shopping or walking down the street. This is a great way to get the message you're repeating into your subconscious. It's also great for stilling that internal voice. You know the first time I tried this, I was really blown away: I think I'm a pretty positive guy, but I was really amazed at how much negative commentary was running through my head all the time. I was never even aware of it until the day I tried this technique, and became aware for the first time when I *didn't* hear it.

VARIATION C—MEDITATING ON THE MEANING

Get into your meditative state, and begin to repeat your mantra, but this time, really focus on the meaning of the words. For example, if you choose "I am" think about each word. "I"—who really is that? Who else could it be? What makes up "I"? What isn't "I"? Who isn't "I"? Now think about the word "am." Am what? What constitutes that? What doesn't constitute that? How is "I" am? How do you know? How can you be sure? Then put it together "I am." How does the meaning change when you put these together? Questioning is a conscious process, but when you really focus and spend time on it, your subconscious will get into the act. Remember that your subconscious likes to operate on its own time-table, so even if you don't emerge from your meditations with new insights, don't be surprised if new insights from your efforts occasionally spring up while you're doing other things. If you're really looking for insights, put time into it when you're doing it, and then don't even think about it until your next session. Paradoxically, if you don't expect specific results, you'll probably be surprised with what you do find.

VARIATION D—PRAYER

There is so much information about prayer, and it is so personal and so specific to each tradition, that it's almost out of the scope of this book. Some of the things that should be considered are that you should do it in an environment where you won't be distracted and can fully focus. Whatever method you do, have it clearly in your mind, and follow it in a way that lets you focus to help you get fully centered into the moment. Authorities on prayer usually recommend doing it in a manner full of faith and confidence in the moment and the outcome, and in a non-needy way. This would make the prayer process elicit a state of faith & confidence generally, rather than emptiness and lack.

MEDITATION 13—FOCUS ON A VISUALIZATION FOR CHANGE

Pictures are interesting. Even if you're not a particularly visual person, I'll bet there's something that you've seen that made you feel really good—or really bad. Maybe grossed out, inspired? Hungry? I don't know about you, but when I see a picture of a hot-fudge sundae, my cravings totally take over! Even if I restrain myself from having one, the sensations just seems to stick in my mind for so long.

Pictures can make you feel things.

Some pictures mean things. A symbol might represent something, like the flag of your nation. There are symbols that represent concepts— like the Yin-Yang symbol, which represents the forces of creation, or symbols that represent a model of the heavenly forces, like the Shri Yantra of the India.

The Indian Shri Yantra and the Chinese Tao (Yin -Yang) symbol.

Some pictures represent complicated chunks of feelings and information, like religious symbols, such as the Christian Cross or the Star of David.

Some pictures represent qualities that you'd like to have. Does a picture of James Bond have any significance to you? Or Marilyn Monroe? Patti Smith? Bruce Lee? George Washington? What traits do your heroes have? What would it be like for you to have them, too?

The following is a visualization exercise that utilizes a picture of some quality that you'd like to have. If you're a runner, for example, you might want to find a picture of a great Olympic athlete that inspires you, or a picture of a fast animal, maybe a zebra or a jaguar.

It's a classic religious tradition, both Eastern and Western, to use the image of a saint or other religious figure in just this way—visualizing the saint and the qualities that figure embodies.

If you're a musician, find a picture of Pavarotti, Keith Moon, or Michael Jackson, or whoever inspires you most. It's got to someone who really *excites* you. Classical pianists traditionally had a little bust of Mozart on their pianos just for inspiration.

FOR ACHIEVING PERSONAL CHANGE

Think of a picture of an animal, an object, or a person, or anything that embodies a characteristic you want to have for yourself. You don't want to become that person or that thing, and you don't have to, since you're a better *you* than they could ever be, but you can *have* that quality that they have.

Some qualities you may wish to improve within yourself:

Patience

Power

Success

Achievement

Calmness

Thinness

Physical Fitness

Creativity

Focus

Spirituality

Sexiness

Cleverness

Musical skill

Strength

Attractiveness

Take your time, use your imagination, even allow your intuition to jump in and offer suggestions. Find the picture in a book, magazine, or online, wherever you can, that really embodies the quality you want. When you have it and it feels right (you may feel an excitement about this exercise), it's time to get started.

Many of us would like to improve several different aspects of ourselves. For the following exercises, it's best to focus on one specific trait at a time, and work with that until you get good results. It's useful to make a little list of the traits to develop, and prioritize them based on how important they are, and also how easily they can be achieved. When starting out on a new technique like this one, it can be helpful to start with a goal that's simpler and easier to achieve, and then going on to bigger ones.

Once you've narrowed down your list, examine your chosen trait. It's not uncommon that when you examine your desired goal closely, it can actually be broken down further into two or more different traits. Reduce your goal down to its simplest part, and work on that. Often, when you begin to achieve one part, other parts will naturally fall into place. If you have been working this technique for a while and you're not making headway, you might want to reexamine your goal and break it down a little further.

(For you record keepers, this will be a combination of **Meditation 10, Visualization**, and **Meditation 11, Feelings**).

1) Assume your favorite sitting posture. Get comfortable and relaxed. Have your picture handy.

2) Control your breathing until it comes naturally, and you don't have to think about it.

3) Look at your picture. Notice everything you can notice about it. Color, shape, texture, size. Connect to the quality that picture embodies, and the way that picture makes you feel. Fix that image in your head, and bring that feeling inside you. When you've got it, shut your eyes.

4) Put all your attention into imagining that you can see that thing in your mind's eye. Notice all the details. Feel that feeling inside you.

5) Be aware of how that image, and that feeling, can change you in a good way, in the right way, in the way that's best for you. Be strong. Be in control.

6) After a while you may find your feelings changed in a better way. If you want to, open your eyes and look at the picture again. Sometimes new insights will emerge. Close your eyes and repeat the above.

7) When you're sure you've got the whole thing, hold it for as long as you can.

8) When you feel it's time to stop, end the meditation.

9) Look around at some different things around you to ground yourself.

A lot of people find a positive feeling from this the first time they do it, and it works even better when you practice it for a while, and really internalize the feelings and images. Remember to start with little goals and work your way up for faster results.

You can use an inspirational image to inspire change in yourself, and you can gradually allow the feelings you're developing to infuse into yourself. If you're developing a particular skill for a particular task, like art or sports, then take a minute just before you engage in that activity to bring the picture, and the feeling, to mind. As you do, you'll be infused with the feeling you're developing. The more you do it, the stronger it gets.

You know, there are some people who feel that if you strongly visualize a thing you want to have or have happen strongly enough and long enough for it to become a part of you, then it has to eventually come into your life. I don't know if that works of not, but if you want to, give it a try!

MEDITATION 14—MIRROR GAZE

The following will give you a strong confident appearance and presence, in addition to being calming and focusing.

You're going to need a mirror at eye level. Maybe you have a small mirror you can put on a table; just be sure it's big enough to see your whole face in. A pocket mirror won't do.

You could also stand in front of a full-length mirror or a bathroom mirror.

MIRROR MEDITATION VARIATION A

When you first do this exercise, look into the mirror and at your own eyes. Pick either the left one or the right one. By picking one eye, you develop a level gaze and avoid the habit of flickering back and forth from left to right that many people have. After you've used one eye for some time, change to the other eye and see if there's any sort of difference. Really look deeply into your own pupil, and try not to blink. Without moving your eyes or allowing much blinking, you will gradually also become aware of the rest of your face, too, but pay attention to your pupils. Do notice your facial expression. It should be calm, peaceful, and neutral. Don't look fierce! Hold that for as long as you can. (It's not uncommon for you to see your reflection change around your eyes in the mirror. This is just your mind playing tricks on you, but if the images are really uncomfortable for you, don't force yourself. Do **Meditation 6** instead, and come back to this later. Don't let anything, even your own imagination, let you lose your cool!)

Try this for five minutes the first time, and then go up to 10 or 15 minutes.

The funny thing about this exercise is that after doing it for a while, you'll find yourself making eye contact with other people more easily, and your confidence level may increase.

VARIATION B—A WARM SMILE

This is similar to the above, but this time I'd like you to hold a *calm, fun smile and feel the feeling of "fun" in your heart* (**Meditation 11**, holding an emotional state, is very good preparation for this one). Hold it, looking in the mirror for as long as you can. Feel that fun smile in your heart, on your face, and especially in your eyes for 5-10 minutes a day. This takes a little longer than the first mirror exercise, but you'll be surprised how, with practice, it not only changes your mood, but you can make others smile with a glance. Keep at it!

VARIATION C—A CONFIDENT GAZE

Now here's an exercise specifically for developing a strong gaze. It uses a mirror.

Place the mirror about three feet on front of you. You should be able to stare right into your own eyes easily. Just look into your own eyes, and see how long you can hold it without blinking. Really hold it for as long as you can. Don't force, or try to look powerful. Just look. While you're doing this, *hold the word "confidence" in your head, and the feeling it gives you,* as you look into your eye. That's what you want to convey, and that's what you will convey. You can also try it with a smile. It will have a positive effect on people as long as you don't try to intimidate (but you could do that, too!)

MEDITATION 15—EXPANDING YOUR PERIPHERAL VISION

This is a very calming meditation that can quickly clear your mind and open you up to the possibilities around you. It's something that a lot of martial artists come by naturally or by deliberate practice, and with good reason. It's also used in shamanic practices. The Hawaiian priests & mystics, who are called Kahuna, call this kind of practice "Hakalau."

Let me tell you something very unusual about the human field of vision here. The center of your field of vision tends to be more connected to your conscious mind, the analytical part. Your peripheral vision, the view around the edges, tends to be connected more with the subconscious mind. That's why something moving into your peripheral vision tends to elicit an instinctive reaction more easily. Think of a bird suddenly flying into your view from behind you. You may react instinctively by turning to look.

This meditation is a good way to click quickly into your subconscious mind.

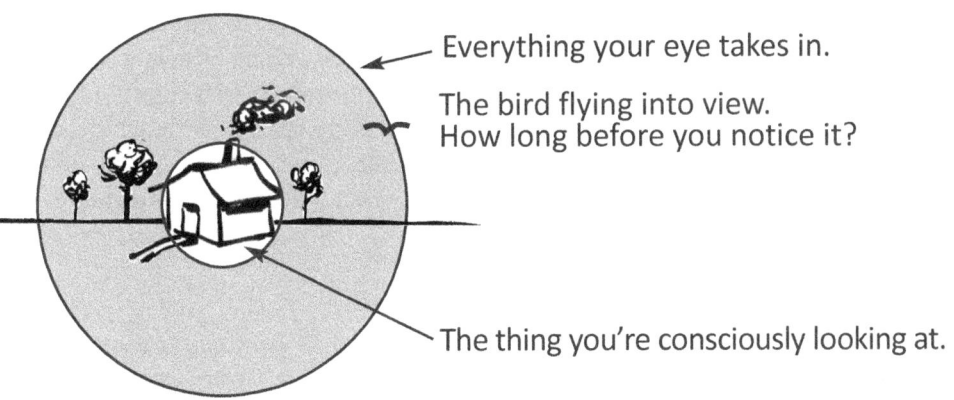

Field of view diagram

It goes like this:

1) Stand and look at a something in front of you at eye level. It doesn't really matter what it is, as long as it doesn't move. If you are outside, you can use a tree or even the horizon line.

2) Fix the center of your gaze at that object.

3) Without moving your eyes or anything at all, just allow your attention to expand to the area surrounding the center of your vision. Notice specific things at the edges of your vision, while keeping the focus of your eyes straight at the thing you're looking at. (The first couple of times you do this, you can extend your arms out at your sides, so you can just barely see the tips of your fingers, left and right).

4) Expand your vision a little more. Don't move your eyes, your head, or anything! While you're looking at the thing in front of you, pay attention to the things at the outer most fringes of your vision—up, down, left, right—all at the same time (If you have your arms extended out to your sides, move your arms further back. See how far you can go without losing sight of both hands.)

5) Expand your vision as much as you can. When you've gone as far as possible, hold it. How does that feel?

6) Finish after a few minutes.

This one is kinda trancy by nature, and a quick way to quiet the mind and open to everything around you. If it helps, imagine being a hunter in the woods or a tiger crouching in tall grass, looking for prey, sitting in stillness and being aware of both left and right simultaneously. Martial artists like this exercise because it allows them to respond quickly and instinctively to their opponents while staying relatively calm and in control. After you practice it a while, try practicing it when you're walking, and then try it with other activities. See how it changes your perceptions!

Extend your arms out to your sides, with your first finger extended. Look straight forward. Can you see both finger tips at the same time? If not, slowly move them forward, until you can. With practice, you'll be able to broaden your field of vision, and bring those fingers way back.

MEDITATION 16—FOCUS ON A FEELING AS A "RESOURCE STATE"

If you've been practicing the meditation that uses a mantra, a prayer, or visualization, you know that there's more to it than just being a mental copy machine, doing automatic repetitions. As you relax into the object of your meditation, there's often also a *feeling* that arises with it. Maybe it's the feeling that led you to choose a particular object for your focus, or maybe it's the feelings that develop from the activity.

Imagine what it would be like if you could bring up any emotional state instantly, when the situation calls for it. For example, say your least-loved Aunt Bertha shows up at your doorstep for a surprise visit at Christmas time. Not only can your meditation techniques help you stay calm and unfazed, but you'll be able to bring up some genuine happiness (albeit from inside yourself) at her surprise appearance. It'll make everybody's Christmas more fun for everybody, and if you're able to keep yourself centered and cool, you might be surprised to find that you even understand Aunt Bertha a little bit better, and why she does these things. She's really not so bad, is she? Well, you'll be the judge of that.

Many of the practices of meditation are aimed at achieving mental peace and calmness, but it's important to be in touch with our feelings, too. Feelings give meaning to everything in human life, and without them, people would be little more than talking adding-machines. The successful practice of meditation should give you more emotional choices.

Exploring feelings in a meditation can give you insights into those feelings and what they mean to you, and with practice, you can access these states for your advantage. The science of Neuro Linguistic Programming, which is a therapeutic system based on several different, direct styles of therapy including hypnosis, pays particular attention to learning to access and cultivate particular emotional states for positive changes. They call a good emotional state that you can use for your benefit a "resource state," since you use it as a resource.

There are several good ways to use the following meditation:

Pick a particular emotion you'd like to start working with. Happiness is a very good one. Always choose positive ones and avoid working with negative emotional states. Not only will they make you feel bad, but they can have negative effects on your health. Meditation won't lower your blood pressure if you're focusing on anger.

For this meditation, we're going to explore the feeling itself. This can be an intense meditation for some people, since feelings, memories and other thoughts are often very intertwined. Keep in mind that the purpose of this and all the meditations in this book are for increased calmness, focus and centeredness. If you find that this or any exercise is making you feel uncomfortable, or bringing up unpleasant feelings or memories, simply stop, get up and move around a little bit and, if you want to, start again, or take a break and try again later.

This time, we're going to focus on a feeling, an emotion, all by itself.

Feelings are funny things. They seem simple enough on the surface, but there's always a little bit more to them. Take happiness, for example. Chances are, some part of you is saying, "happiness? I know what happiness is!" but think about happiness for a second. I bet you feel more than one kind of happiness. There's the kind of happiness you might feel after you've done a job really well. Is it the same happiness you feel when you get a happy surprise? And is that happiness the same kind you feel when eating your favorite food? Or is it the kind of happiness your feel from being at peace with yourself and the world? Happiness comes in many different flavors. There are different words for all these sensations, and each person has their own words to describe their own particular states. You might use the word "satisfaction" to describe what I call "contentment." I might say "delightful" for something that you'd call "terrific." It doesn't matter what the word is, as long as you know what it means for you. I now invite you to pick a particular emotion and try it on for a short span of time.

1) Assume your favorite sitting position. Get comfortable and relaxed.

2) Control your breathing until it comes naturally, and you don't have to think about it.

3) Ready? Turn your attention to the feeling of your choice .

4) Close your eyes and focus on it. Really study it. Where is it coming from? What is it like when it's really strong? What makes you feel this way? Allow it to grow and develop. What new learning can you get from it?

5) When you have the desired feeling strong and distinct, just the way you'd like it to be, hold onto it.

6) Repeat steps four and five, perhaps 6-10 times.

7) Then clear your mind afterward, by thinking about something totally different, pleasant but neutral, like the smell of bread baking or football scores. Finish, open your eyes, and take a deep breath.

If you're an actor or a public speaker, or even an athlete, this is a great exercise for maximizing your potential. And with a little practice, this can also be a very powerful technique for change.

APPLICATIONS

Future activities: Imagine a situation in your immediate future, maybe a job interview or a date, or a project you've been meaning to work on. Hold it in your head as you bring up the emotion you've been practicing, and flood that date or that interview with the chosen feeling. (I'm going to assume happiness is your choice, but if the activity is a dinner with an annoying relative, like Aunt Bertha, you might want to imagine peace and tolerance.) See yourself in the situation, and feel the chosen feeling. Imagine it affecting any and all other people in the situation, all for the best. Even see the environment positively affected by it. Play it all the way through, like a movie in your mind, and be sure the feeling brings about your desired outcome. Play it through several times, in different ways and always flood it with your desired emotion. I'm betting that you will be in your best possible state when you really go into that situation.

Past experiences: Memories consist of two parts. There's the **fact** of the memory, what actually happened, and the **emotion** attached to it. Now you can't change the fact that a thing happened, but you can change the emotion attached to it. Think about it. For the most part, emotions surrounding memories fade over time. They're still there to some degree, but the emotional intensity you felt about something, like your teddy bear's birthday, has probably faded somewhat since you were a kid. Sometimes something happens in our past that has strong emotional connotations that don't fade over time. They stay powerful and influence our future. If the emotion is a positive, useful one, use it as a resource state. Negative states don't make good resource states.

If you have a past experience with a bad feeling or connotation attached to it, you can try this exercise. (Of course, for powerful, negative issues, you should definitely seek the help of a professional, like a psychologist, hypnotherapist, or NLP practitioner.) First, isolate and build up your positive resource state in the same way we described. Then hold that positive resource strongly, while "playing" the difficult memory in your mind, as if it were a movie. If the positive resource state is strong, it'll defuse the bad feelings associated with the memory.

> I knew a woman who always had trouble speaking in public, but her job required it. She explained that, in high school, she gave a talk in front of class, but her shirt was buttoned sideways. I don't know whether the class noticed, but she did—after the fact. Every time she speaks in public she thinks of it, and gets flustered and humiliated. By reviewing that memory, but strongly holding the emotion of good-natured humor instead of embarrassment, she was finally able to laugh at herself and neutralize the embarrassment.

Self Exploration: Pick a feeling and go with it. The longer you hold it, the more insights may come up. This is a good one when you're looking for inspiration.

Anchoring a resource state for future use: Pick your desired feeling and use your meditation to generate that feeling inside you until it's good and strong. As it reaches its full strength, execute a gesture to "anchor" it by setting that gesture as a trigger. For example, let's say you want to create a trigger, or "anchor," for a state of confidence. In your meditation, you develop the feeling of confidence, and at the point where the feeling is really strong, you pinch your thumb and index finger together and hold it for a few seconds while feeling the feeling. Repeat the process several times, and soon you'll begin to find that every time you do your anchor gesture, you'll feel the desired emotional state of confidence coming to you.

Imagine that, sometime later, you go to a job interview. Just as you enter the office, you fire the trigger (pinch your fingers together) for confidence. You may be surprised to find how really confident you feel. You can anchor any kind of feeling or memory. It just takes practice (think of the way certain songs always make you feel a certain way, or remind you of something special. This is the same anchor effect). This effect is commonly used in hypnosis and Neuro Linguistic Programming to enable people to access more emotional tools and resources.

MEDITATION 17—CHAKRAS

Perhaps you've already heard of chakras. There's an enormous amount of information about chakras in books and on the Web. There's so much that you could spend the rest of your life studying them. This is going to be a very basic overview, but sufficient to get you on your way.

"Chakra" literally means wheel, and suggests a sense of motion or spinning, as opposed to a circle, which could be static. A chakra is a certain specific location within the body which is believed to be an energy center. There are considered to be many chakras within the body and each energy center deals with a particular kind of energy and is related to a different bodily area. Interestingly, different schools of thought may disagree about where the chakras are, what they do, and what color they are. They are often depicted as lotus flowers with different numbers of petals. Like flowers, they open and bloom when properly attended to.

I'm going to use one of the most common arrangements, often called the "rainbow chakra system." It's called that because the chakras are arranged according to the colors of the rainbow. If you decide to look into this further, you'll find more specific, and maybe different, instruction. Use what makes the most sense to you. I've used this for a long time and I find it works nicely for me.

BUT FIRST—AN INTERESTING EXPERIMENT

When dealing with things like energy centers in the body, it's worth discussing the theory of energy. To modern Western thought, the mind communicates with every part of the body via the nervous system, like a kind of "electrical wiring" which transmits tiny electrochemical signals. Classical far-Asian thought about this is that an energy, *chi,* or *ki,* which runs along a series of "meridians." In the philosophy of India and East Asia, they call it *prana,* and it runs along a series of "nadis" (energy paths) into centers called "chakras." Who's right? Does one system really exist over the others? Is it all a lot of hooey? Hard to say. Energy centers aren't distinct solid structures the way organs are, and the jury's still out about the whole energy issue. But I say, if it works, and it sure seems to, use it!

Now here's the experiment: there's believed to be a chakra right in the middle of the palm of the hand. We're going to try and charge it. I want you to sit comfortably, and look at the palm of your hand. Try it with the hand you *don't* write with first. Get into a comfortable and meditative state and stare at the place right in the middle of your hand. Imagine focusing all the energy of your body into this one place. Imagine the energy of your body running down your arm and right into this point. Try it for about three minutes. Are you feeling anything? Many people will begin to feel a tingling or a warmth at that point or close to it. If you don't feel anything, try it again, or try the other hand. Is it energy, or just a suggestion you're feeling? I don't know for sure, it could be either, or both. The masters say "energy flows where attention goes."

We're going to get into a meditative state and imagine getting familiar with each of the chakras and energizing them. We're going to do this with a calm energy, charging them with the calm feeling that we're developing with our other meditation practices.

THE CHAKRAS WE'LL USE ARE AS FOLLOWS *(From the bottom up)*:

Root—At the perineum, the place between your anus and your genitalia. Its color is **red** (Also called the **Mulhadara**)

Sexual—In the center of the pelvis, behind the genitals. Its color is **orange (Svadhisthana)**

Belly—An inch below the belly button. Its color is **yellow (Manipura)**

Heart—In the center of the chest. Its color is **green (Anahata)**

Throat—At the base of the throat. Its color is **blue (Vishuddha)**

"Third eye"—Right between the eyebrows. Its color is **Purple (Ajna)**

Top of the head—at the very top point of the head, or even a little higher above. Its color is **white**, and, like white light, is considered to be a conglomeration of all the other colors (Also called the **Sahasrara** Chakra)

BLOCKAGES IN THE ENERGY FLOW

Chakras can become tense under emotional stress just the way a muscle can become tense. During the course of this sort of meditation, you may come across "blockages." They may feel like tightness, stiffness, or stuckness, or occasionally another form or discomfort. Sometimes these blockages are the result of physical stress or inactivity. Some blockages have an emotional component, usually resulting from an emotional overload or a repressed feeling. Have you ever been in a situation where you really wanted to say or do something, but you just couldn't?

If you remember the stuck feeling in your stomach that came with that, then you know what I'm talking about. When that stuck feeling is held for a long time, you body "learns" to do it automatically.

As you imagine the energy flowing into and through these places, and just begin to focus your attention on these places, they begin to loosen and open up. You can also massage these places, do stretches and yoga, or just work them loose in your mind. Very occasionally, focusing on these spots might begin to make them feel tighter and more blocked. If that's the case, stop. Get up, try stretching, massage or physical exercise, and explore it again later, maybe with a different 'feeling" of energy.

The Chakras

Top of the Head	Color: WHITE (Sahasrara)
"Third Eye"	Color: PURPLE (Ajna)
Throat	Color: BLUE (Vishhuddha)
Heart	Color: GREEN (Anahata)
Belly	Color: YELLOW (Manipura)
Sexual	Color: ORANGE (Svadhisthana)
Root	Color: RED (Mulhadara)

Consider the blockage and whether there's some sort of a message from your subconscious there for you. When these blockages have been created from some sort of emotional conflict, you may find those emotions being released as they become unblocked. It may feel like an unburdening, or a freedom.

When you start exploring the chakras, use about 6-12 breaths at each, and then move on to the next. As you get familiar with them, you can spend more time if you like.

Let's begin.

1) Assume your sitting position. Get comfortable and get your breathing deep, and peaceful and regular.

2) Move your attention to the lowest chakra, your root chakra. Imagine a peaceful red light charging the point at your perineum, the point between your anus and your genitalia. Let the glow expand freely. Don't force it. If you feel any tension at this point or in the area immediately surrounding it, imagine relaxing and loosening it. Allow all the tension to fade. Imagine energy rising up into it from the Earth. 6-12 breaths.

3) Raise your attention up your spine to your second chakra. This one is related to sexual energy. Charge it with an orange glow, and let it expand for 6-12 breaths. Some people find this point somewhat blocked for a variety of reasons. If you do, work on opening and releasing any blockages.

4) Raise your attention up to the point in the base of your belly. Charge this point with a warm yellow light. Let the glow expand outwards, 6-12 breaths. This point may already be relaxed and open from your other breathing practices, but if you feel any blockages allow them to open naturally.

5) Raise your inner attention upwards to the point at your heart. Charge it with a warm green light. Let that glow expand outward. If you feel any blockages allow them to open. 6-12 breaths.

6) Raise your attention upward to the base of your throat. Charge this point with a blue light, and let it expand outward. This is your communication chakra, charging and relaxing it is considered to help your communication abilities. If you feel tightness or blockages, relax and expand them. 6-12 breaths.

7) Raise your attention to your "third eye" point between your eyebrows. Charge it with a beautiful purple energy, and allow that to expand outward. If you feel any dizziness, or other odd feelings, use less energy or effort. Go easy and gradually. 6-12 breaths.

8) Raise your attention to a point a few inches above the top of your head. There's no color here, but some people like to imagine an expanding ball of white light. Let the light expand and imagine it lighting any shadows that might exist in your imagination or your surroundings. Bask in the pure glow. 6-12 breaths.

9) Finish by moving your attention back downward. Some people stop at the third chakra (yellow, belly chakra) others go all the way down the body through the first chakra (red, base chakra), and into the earth. Take a deep breath and stand up and shake out your arms and legs.

How did that feel? This can be a very interesting exercise, and regular practice will certainly pay off. After a few sessions, you'll very likely be able to detect blockages, if you have any. Now, if you feel any undue pressure in these places, or you feel sudden anger or any other odd feelings or emotions, either stop for a while or practice less energetically. Don't be too anxious for results, If there are blockages, it's a gradual process and a natural one, and you have all the time you need to succeed at your own pace. This exercise, when done correctly, will leave you feeling terrific, peaceful, and energized.

> I began doing this exercise about 15 years ago. At that time, I had a big bunch of friends, but sometimes, when I was with them, I felt more like an entertainment director for the group than a friend to any of them. It was like they were each pulling me in a different direction. Several of them actually made me feel drained just by being around them, and after a while I felt like I was almost dissolving, and I also found myself feeling really depressed. I never thought about it before, but I knew immediately I needed to be more centered. I began practicing this meditation, focusing especially on my third chakra, which is considered to be the "center" point, and I needed to feel centered. It took a little while, but I began to feel changes. For me, that third chakra did make me feel more centered. But it didn't stop there. The root chakra helped me feel more grounded, and helped me realize that it was better to spend less time with those friends. That left me feeling less drained. I enjoyed the solidity and the control I was feeling, and it got even better. My heart chakra, which at first felt solid and almost rock-like, began to open. I remember the feeling being like a fleece jacket around my chest unrolling gradually. I hadn't realized that I'd been blocking a lot of feelings. As I let it out gradually, I actually felt kind of rotten, but over a number of sessions the "fleece jacket" opened. When it was gone, I found I wasn't feeling so bad. In fact, it felt kind of nice. One day, sitting alone in my living room, in the middle of my meditation, I moved my attention to my heart chakra, and I heard a kind of a giggling. I realized it was me! I was giggling! My heart chakra tickled! Over the following years I learned how to charge that chakra to feel good, even when the chips were down. It's not a cure all—when bad things happen I still feel them, but it's a very useful resource to have.

I don't know what this meditation can do for you, but I hope you get wonderful results from it!

MEDITATION 18—EMPTY YOUR MIND FOR PROBLEM SOLVING AND INSPIRATION

"I wish someone would just tell me the answer!"

Did you ever think or even say that? Maybe you were trying to remember where you left your keys, or trying to figure out how to finish a term paper, or you were presented with a situation that just didn't make any sense. Maybe it made you want to bang your head against the wall!

Mystics seeking answers have been using meditation to find those answers for centuries. In fact, if you've been exploring meditation in other places, you've probably come across stories like these over and over again. They illustrate "meditation for seeking answers," "meditation to seek wisdom," "meditation to find yourself," and so forth.

It sounds very mystical, but there's good psychological science behind it. First of all, scientists have discovered that learning is "state dependent," and by *state*, they mean mental or emotional state. The things you learn in a particular mental or emotional state tend to be best recalled when you're in that same state. For example, when you're happy, your mind will most easily access information that came into it at those times that you were happy. When you're angry, you'll most easily remember things that happened when you were angry. Anyone who's had a fight with a spouse or close relative will know that if you get them angry, or they do it to you, every other instance that resulted in anger suddenly pops into mind. Your subconscious mind, which is in charge of filing away every bit of information that ever came into your head, creates a lot of different kinds of cross-references, and emotional states are one kind of organizational system.

Did you ever have the experience of studying for an important exam in calm and peace, and when you went into the exam room, you got nervous and your mind blanked? That's an example of *state dependency*. If you had studied in the same kind of environment that you were taking the test in, you'd have an easier time remembering. You might not have gotten so nervous. And the guy who breezed through the exam? Most likely he didn't get nervous, and so he was able to access a state similar to the one he was in when he studied.

Before the breakup of the Soviet Union, the Communists put enormous resources behind their Olympic athletes, and one of their big findings was all about state dependent learning. Olympic athletes practice for hours every day, of course, and they usually begin practice in the afternoons or evenings, typically after their classes or jobs. Most of the competitions, however, are all-day affairs that begin early in the morning. They discovered that by training their athletes *at the same time* that the competitions were scheduled, the athletes were really at the top of their game. So, when they knew a particular competition would be at 8:00am, they'd be sure that for at least a few weeks before the match, the athlete would be training at the same time as the competition. In that way, their physical state during competition was precisely the same as was is in practice, and they access all their skills more effectively.

I can tell you that when I was a competitive fencer, I trained from 6:00pm to about 1:30am nearly every day of the week. I was not at my best at an 8:00am competition no matter how well trained I was or how much sleep I got the night before. Wish I knew about those studies back then!

How does state dependent learning relate to you? I already described the way your subconscious mind organizes memories according to the state you're in. Now, let's say you're looking for those missing car keys. All you have to do is remember what mental state you were in, and you'll remember where those keys are, right? Sounds simple enough—*if* you remember what state you were in. Retracing your steps can help, because it also usually reminds you what you were thinking while you were in the process of losing those keys so well. But what if you can't get yourself into the same state, or you just don't remember what you were feeling? If you try emptying your mind, it just may come to you.

Here's why: Because your subconscious mind organizes your thoughts according to mental states, any particular mental state you're in tends to act like a filter to your thoughts. If you're in a happy state, you're telling your subconscious mind to make available all those thoughts related to happiness, your happiness. Moreover, you're also telling it to only accept thoughts that can be filed under "happy," and put away any thoughts that aren't classified to your mind as happy ones. Did you ever have a day where you felt so good that nothing could bring you down? You just felt good, and everything you came across in the day either was also good in some way, or you just didn't want to deal with it. Maybe you just didn't even notice it. Maybe you know someone who's always down, and not only can they share a history of bad memories and failed adventures, but everything that comes to them seems to be rotten? Could be a voodoo curse, or it could be that their subconscious is filtering out all the good stuff and only presenting them with crap. They've got their "unhappy filter" on. Your emotional states act like filters for both the past and the present, and in that way, your mental state really does affect your life.

All very fascinating and useful, but it still doesn't tell us where the car keys are. Here's the thing: If there's no emotional state, you're telling your subconscious to access everything—telling it not to filter anything out.

That's one of the reasons why so many esoteric circles recommend kinds of "empty-mind" meditations. Not only does the emotion*less* state allow the mind to access more of your memories, it also allows it to *cross-reference* much more material. There's an awful lot of information in your cranium, and a great deal of inspiration comes from the ability to put bits of the known together in new unknown ways. Anyone who's worked with creative types such as artists, musicians, and writers knows that even though "new, young" talent gets a lot of the attention, it's usually the older folks that really come up with the most creative materials. "Inspiration" is based on experience far more than anyone guesses.

Now, many proponents of the "empty-the-mind" meditations say that the practitioner is opening his mind up to so much more, and I feel that is true, too. On the most immediate level, you can become aware of everything you're not normally aware of when you're walking and talking during the course of your day. Many also feel that you are opened up to even more subtle influences and inspirations from outside yourself. I can't say much for sure about this, but if you feel you've ever experienced this, or you're curious to try to experience it, this is a good way to start. I'll give a few examples of this following the meditation. Let's get started.

This is very similar to **Meditation 4**, Emptying the Mind, so if you've been practicing that, you'll feel very comfortable with this. The main difference is that, before you begin, you will state your goal clearly to yourself.

Have a clear goal in mind, whether it's remembering something, or finding an answer to a question, or getting an inspiration. Make it fairly specific—give your subconscious a good hint to follow. You can say it aloud 3-4 times, or write it on a card and read it several times, and put it in front of you.

1) Assume your favorite sitting position. Be sure you're comfortable, and you won't be disturbed for a few minutes, and your back is straight.

2) Close your eyes.

3) Now, relax. If you want to, use the tense-and-relax method from Chapter 7. Or just allow your body to unwind by itself.

4) Breathe in the way we practiced—slowly and deeply. Do this for a few moments until everything about you is calm and still.

5) Turn your attention inwards, and tune out any sensations outside of you. Remember that if there's an emergency, you will still always be able to respond instantly.

6) Think of stillness and solidness. As if your body were as still as a mountain, or a tree in a quiet forest, a forest without wind or movement of any kind. Just quiet peace.

7) Expand the feeling of stillness in your body, and in your head.

8) Hold the peaceful stillness.

9) During the stillness, thoughts may begin to come up into your awareness. Most of the time, these thoughts are the ones your subconscious has been working with, just under the level of your conscious mind. Some are just memories of things that happened in the last day or so, or thoughts that were percolating in the back of your mind. Sometimes the answer you're seeking, if it's something like those missing car keys, will pop up immediately. If you have the answer you're looking for, you're done. Otherwise, just hold onto the stillness and let those sensations go. With practice, your control over the stillness will strengthen, like a muscle.

10) Eventually, you'll move past those "under-the-surface" thoughts, and you'll find a deeper stillness. Just hold that state of no-state for a while. It should feel very good and relaxed. The answer you're seeking may not make itself apparent—you may not notice anything at all. That's actually fine. Just hold the no-state state for a while. Don't think, don't analyze. Just be.

11) Eventually it'll seem like it's time to finish, open your eyes, and be aware of the feelings within you and around you. Give yourself a few minutes to come back up to full waking speed.

When you do this, don't be surprised if you don't find the information you're seeking during the meditation, and don't be surprised if it just pops into your head suddenly, sometime within or about the next 24 hours, either. That's the way the subconscious works. Very likely, you've already had the experience of trying to figure something out, giving up, and finding it pop into your mind shortly after. What we're doing with this meditation is simply training your mind to have this available and under your control.

The key element to this meditation is to have your goal *clear* in your mind when you start. Emptying your mind allows it to put its full force to the question. The thoughts that come up after the initial clearing of your head are things that your subconscious is working with in some way. Occasionally, deeper, more intense, more emotional issues might come up in the course of this meditation. Usually that's your mind telling you of the importance of these things. If they are very disturbing, stop the meditation. Your mind might be telling you these things are more important to deal with first. Consider what your mind is offering you, perhaps even that you should ask for help to deal with them. Your goal is to have control over your mind, but also to take good care of yourself. Don't neglect these thoughts if they keep coming up, but don't let them dominate you either.

SLEEP

You can also do a variation of this in your sleep! Just before bed, say or read aloud your clearly defined goal 3-4 times. If you want, put it under your pillow, and go to sleep. You may find the answer you're seeking in the morning, or sometime during the day.

Longer courses of meditation are good for weightier, more philosophical issues, and for generally clearing your head and opening up to inspiration.

METAPHYSICS

This sort of mental clearing is also used by many psychics and mystics, to open up their more subtle sensitivities. You can exercise this to whatever degree you believe in it, and I suspect the greater your belief, the greater your results. Please note that your mind may well play tricks on you if you harbor any strong feelings about this. For example, if you are really strongly seeking angel communications, you may get them, but your subconscious, in its desire to serve your conscious mind, may provide some phony messages. To the same degree, if you're focusing on a fear of scary ghosts, your subconscious mind may give you those too! Whether you seek missing car keys or higher consciousness, be aware that if you get scary, silly, or just peculiar messages, always follow common sense. If a voice in your imagination tells you to do something that you wouldn't do if another person suggested it, it's probably better to chalk it up to your subconscious misinterpreting your needs.

INTUITION

Intuition is a funny thing. It may seem magical, even to the person experiencing it, but so much of it is actually made up of your subconscious mind drawing logical conclusions based on its vast collection of information. At the same time, it may well be that you are also opening your mind to outside information on a more subtle level. To get an intuitive reading on something or someone, get into your meditative state, empty and open your mind to all the possibilities of the thing you're reading and see what comes to you.

With practice, you can get into your meditative state very quickly and casually, even on the fly.

Some fortune tellers and card-readers use their cards or crystal balls as rough signposts, and then use their intuition to give them more information. Real fortune tellers will tell you that it takes a lot of long, hard practice to get accurate and meaningful information.

EMPATHY

Empathy refers to intuiting people's feelings. I don't know about you, but I've had experiences sitting down next to strangers on the bus and just feeling their emotional state, particularly when it's a very strong one. I don't think I'm particularly sensitive, but I do think that we can sometimes feel what others are feeling. It also seems that the more familiar one person is to another, the more sensitive they are to each other. I used to date a girl who, in her sleep, occasionally dreamt of things that happened to me that she had no way of knowing about, with surprising accuracy. If you want experiment with training your receiving powers, use this empty-mind meditation while holding the *feeling* of the person you want to read. They say the feeling you get from a person is like their psychic email address. (Think of someone you know well, and notice the feeling you have that's unique to them. That's it). Needless to say, if you want to experiment with this, *don't* do it with anyone who has exhibited any sort of mental illness or odd behavior.

The experts say that it is *very important* that after you do this, to "cut the cords" of psychic connection. It's like hanging up the phone. Just imagine that there are wires connecting you to the other person, and that you have scissors or a great big sword or some such, and just slice through the wires. In your imagination, see the cords snapping away like rubber bands.

TELEPATHY

Similar to empathy, but instead of receiving, try sending a message! You'll need a willing partner to practice this with, one who is in a different place than you are. Agree on a particular time for the experiment, so you can both get into a meditative state at the same time, and so afterwards, you can call them to check your findings. You'll use the same meditational technique, but once you've got a strong feeling of the receiver's "psychic address," experiment with strongly *sending* a message. Make it a simple one and repeat it over and over in your mind for about five minutes. Some Indian Yogis who've written about this recommend a very deep meditational state, lying flat in the "corpse position," but not asleep. Remember to cut the cords (see above) after you're done. Good luck!

PSYCHOMETRY

This is a technique whereby one gets impressions from a solid object. By applying the empathy technique, but to an object, the seer tries to get a "read" about the object's owner or its recent history. Again, this is a good one to practice with an open-minded friend or two. Each should bring an old, small, personal object that has a history that they know. They have to know what the history of the object is, so that the reader can check their accuracy afterwards. Each person should take a turn with a different object. The object can be wrapped in paper so the reader can't make guesses, and it is held in the hand of the reader (they say left hand works best). The reader goes into their empty-mind state, and moves their attention into the hand holding the object, similar to the way you moved your attention onto the palm of the hand while preparing for the Chakra meditation (**Meditation 17**). Move your attention to the object, empty your mind and find out what kind of impressions you get. Say your impressions out loud to your partner, and your partner can gently guide you to keep the images flowing by asking you questions, or point you in a direction of thought (without giving too much away) by prompting you with questions about the object and its history. Allow yourself at least 5-10 minutes, since the first impressions may well be from your own subconscious. After you're done, unwrap the object, and compare your findings with what the owner knows about the object. You'll probably find that some impressions are true and some aren't. They say practice makes perfect! Makes sure everybody gets a turn with different objects.

MEDITATION 19—GUIDED MEDITATIONS, OR GUIDED VISUALIZATIONS

Guided Meditations or Guided Visualizations, are something like directed daydreams. The main difference between a daydream and a guided visualization is that the guided one is created with a specific kind of a result in mind, usually a deeply meditative state.

By now, you should know that even if you're not comfortable with "visualizations," it's nothing more than another word for "meditations." Very often, Guided Meditations are called Guided Visualizations but it's pretty much the same.

A daydream, almost by definition, is an indulgence into an emotional state or a fantasy. Some daydreams occupy an idle hour by leading someone into an emotionally pleasurable fantasy. Daydreams are for entertainment purposes.

Occasionally, daydreams can lead a person into a very undesirable emotional state. Did you ever know someone who had an attack of jealousy, depression, or anger as a result of letting their imagination get away from them? They started to think about one thing, and they let it lead them into a place where one undesirable feeling leads to another, until they've drilled themselves down into a really unhappy place. Obviously, this is not a good thing to do as a regular practice, and yet they do it. Maybe we all do sometimes.

On the other hand, the best daydreams leave you with a good feeling, and they exercise your imagination but usually not too much more. But once in a while, you might have a daydream, and find that you get an insight or a solution that just kind of pops up in your mind, either during or after the daydream.

One of the nice things about guided meditation is that, like the previous emptying-the-mind meditation (**Meditation 18**), it takes the emotional constraints off your subconscious, but it does it in a different way. Instead of deliberately quieting the awareness, the technique we're about to learn simply takes the attention away to another place, and allows the subconscious to do its thing, undisturbed. Imagine your conscious mind like a nervous boss who gives an assignment to his employee (the subconscious), but then watches over the employee's shoulder so much that the employee can't get the job done. The guided meditation takes the boss for a little walk in the garden, and allows the employee to get the job done undisturbed.

A guided meditation is like an inner journey, one where you can go anyplace you want to go, and do anything you want to do. Because it takes place inside your mind, you can also choose whether a particular emotional state is important, and what the best way is to gently suggest it to yourself.

Before you begin the next meditation, decide what you want to accomplish. Do you want to access a state of security and relaxation? You can visit a place that's special just for you. Do you want to go to a place where you can develop your skills undisturbed? Do you want to prepare for an upcoming exam, a date or an audition? Any of these are possible! I'll give examples of each of the above, and you can explore them as is, or create your own for your needs.

Guided visualizations make an excellent break from stress, they are a good way to prepare for an upcoming event, and they're good for developing skills and insights. Some people say they are even good for healing.

Sometimes the structure will take the form of a journey you can go on and travel to significant places that you know, or that you create. You can include symbols for things that have meaning to you. You can create desired results for unresolved situations. And like all the other meditations, the more you practice, the stronger and more effective these become.

Who guides this guided meditation? You can, or you can leave it to somebody else. There are many pre-recorded guided meditations that you can buy, or you can make your own. You can record it into a tape-recorder, and play it back to yourself.

As you construct your visualization, you can make it very direct and realistic, and really view the things you want to work on as if they are movies of the real thing. If you prefer, you can make them symbolic and mysterious, almost dreamlike, and use symbols that have meaning only to you. The second sort is called **metaphoric**. A **metaphor** is basically a symbolic representation of something.

Why are these techniques effective? One of Emile Coué's many contributions to the psychology of personal change was "The Law of Reversed Effort." It's like this: many people try to make changes in their life through the use of will power. Will power is powerful indeed, and can work wonders, but equally as often, the more will power a person applies to change, the more resistance they encounter. Think about people who try really hard to stop smoking, or lose weight, or get more exercise. The harder they try the harder it becomes. Coué discovered that changes introduced to the subconscious in a gentle way encounter no resistance. According to this concept, we wouldn't try to command the psyche to make changes. Rather, approach the change gently, and allow the mind to accept the suggestion and run with it. Do you have any doubts whether this is effective? It's the basis of nearly all advertising. A poster on a wall may have a headline that shouts out the command "BUY NOW!" but it's the image of the product on that same poster, when *seen day after day* by the people who pass it by and never *consciously* look at it anymore, that gets planted deeply in the mind and creates the craving.

GUIDED VISUALIZATION FOR RELAXATION AND COMFORT

The goal of this exercise is to get to a state of comfort and relaxation, by going to a place in your imagination that has that meaning for you. I can't suggest what's best for you, but I bet you know one, or you can make one up. But to start with, I'll make one up so you can get the idea.

What does relaxation and comfort mean to you? Where is your place of greatest relaxation and comfort, the place where you feel so totally safe and comfortable that all your cares melt away, and time seems to stand still? For some people it could be the mountains or the beach, or their grandmother's kitchen. If it's a real place, it should be one that has only good, happy memories associated with it. If you prefer, it could be a place from a book or a movie, or just something you created for yourself. You know, for a long time, every time I did this meditation, I could come up with no better location than a favorite old bar in New York, where I spent many happy hours over the years with friends, or just sitting by myself, cozy by the fire, reading a book. I'd imagine the feel of the coarse, beer-soaked tabletops, and the darkened wooden panels, the cool, damp smell of the beer, and burgers charring in the kitchen. It may not be a very traditional image for meditation, like the Taj Mahal or a shaded glen, but I like it.

For this example, I'm going to create a special place of peace and relaxation. It's a grassy field on a hill overlooking the beach. If you prefer some other location, read through the process, and adapt it as you see fit. It's all about you!

VARIATION A—RELAXATION AND INSIGHT

Read through it first. If your memory is good, and you can commit the whole thing to memory, then you can close your eyes & go through it from beginning to end.

If you want to get started in a hurry, read one paragraph, close your eyes and envision what you have just read. When it seems realistic in your imagination, and you've explored it thoroughly, open your eyes and go on to the next paragraph. After a few times you'll be able to do the whole thing from memory.

If you have time to prepare, make a recording from beginning to end, and just relax and play it back to yourself.

You can do this with eyes open or closed, but when we're starting out, let's do it with eyes closed for less distraction. Sit comfortably, and close your eyes.

> Allow yourself to relax. Allow your breathing to get smooth and regular. Relax.
>
> Imagine you're walking on the beach. You can see the waves gently washing up and down the beach to one side of you, and the sky above you. You can hear the shushing of the water as it washes in and out over the sand. You can feel the warmth of the sun on your skin, the sand under your feet, and smell that special sea air smell.
>
> You look up ahead to the horizon, which seems to go on forever. You notice the color of the sand, the sparkle of the sun on the sea, the sound of your steps crunching on the sand, feel a cool spray of water from the waves on your skin, as you feel each step sink slightly into the sand in that way they will. You walk along, enjoying all of these sensations and more, and just taking all the time you need.
>
> As you walk, you begin to notice so much more. The rhythm of the waves, the occasional seagull flying past, and a pebble on the beach. You stop for a moment to pick up the pebble and hold it in your hand. You slip the pebble in your pocket, and then you continue on your walk. Enjoy all the sensations you can see and hear

and feel. With every step, it seems like you are noticing more and more new sensations and awarenesses. What are they? How do they make you feel?

A little way ahead, you notice the hill off to one side. That's your goal, and maybe it makes you happy to see it, maybe even a little excited to be going there. Have you been there before? How long has it been? If you haven't been there before, what are your expectations of it?

You turn toward the hill, and begin to climb up the sandy slope. It's an easy climb, and you enjoy feeling the muscles in your legs moving you, and maybe you're surprised at how quickly you get so high up that little hill. The breezes may become a little stronger as you reach the top, and you see more grass growing there.

A few more steps and you reach the top. The top of the hill is flat and wide and thickly covered with green, green grass. The breezes are strong, but cooling, and the sun shines warmly and bright on the blades of grass. You smell the salty-sweet ocean air, and hear the seagulls cry. You walk forward onto the thick grass, and notice the resilient, spongy feeling of it under your feet, so different from the sand you were walking on a few minutes ago.

You walk around that grassy hilltop for a while, and soon you find yourself in a place that's just right, the most comfortable place of all. The spot that's your special place on the grass. You know when you get to it, because it just feels right. On your spot, you can look around and see the beach and the sea below you, and the blue sky, maybe wispy clouds everywhere above you. You look as far as you can out to sea, so far you can almost imagine you can see over the horizon. Way out to sea you can see a tiny boat, and you hear the call of the distant gulls. When you inhale you enjoy the warm sweet grassy smell. It seems like such a good idea to lie down there.

As soon as your back stretches across the grass, the warmth and softness of it just feels so good to you. So good you might almost want to giggle like a little kid, and maybe you do. Each time you inhale deeply, you can enjoy all those sweet smells, and feel so much better with every breath. You kick your shoes off, if you didn't already, and you wiggle your toes and fingers in the wet grass. You feel so very, very good. You take a breath, so slow and deep and comfortable, and as you exhale you want to say, "Mmmm.." and so maybe you do. Then another just like it, and then another. Mmmm..

It occurs to you that there's nobody around, that you have this place all to yourself, and you can enjoy it for as long as you want. Just like this. You feel so comfortable and so very, very relaxed, and yet you're not at all sleepy. You're enjoying it too much.

As you relax more, you know that this place is a place where you can feel totally relaxed, and totally safe. This is a place where you can expand.... No one and nothing can be here unless you put them here. You have complete control over this place. Mmmm.

You can enjoy this place of total security and comfort for as long as you like. It's your place, and only yours.

At some point, you remember the pebble in your pocket. Your fingers glide across the cool grass and into your pocket. You inhale the green smell and the sea air as your fingers find the pebble, and you lazily pull it out. You feel the texture under your fingers. What does it feel like? Round and smooth, but a little rough, too. Is it warm or cold? Take a look at it. What color is it? Look a little deeper. Have you ever seen that color anywhere else? It seems heavier than you expected, too, doesn't it? Roll it around in your fingers. Enjoy it, and be aware of all the little things about it that you didn't notice before. Sometimes holding an object like this can remind you of something else. What might you be reminded of now? Hold it in your hand, but don't think about it too much.

Lay back and enjoy your private place. You can stay here for as long as you need to, until you feel all those wonderful feelings deep, deep inside you.

When it's the right time to go, stand up and notice how good you feel, how flexible and relaxed and free. And you have this feeling with you, inside you, as you go back down the hillside to the beach.

Walking back on the beach you still have that sense of freedom and security, and the pebble back in your pocket. You walk all the way back up the beach, and as you do, you may notice that you're so much more aware of the color and texture of the sand and the water and the way everything feels.

Time to finish. Breathe deeply, and when you're ready, open your eyes. How do you feel?

Try this when you need a little mental break, or you're mentally stuck for answers, or you need focus or confidence. If you record this on tape or an MP3 to play back for yourself, speak softly and a little slower than you normally would for a more trance-like quality.

VARIATION B—VISUALIZATION FOR DEVELOPING SKILLS

Do you have a skill you'd like to develop? Something you do well that you'd like to do better? Or something you're not yet good at, but would like to do better? Practicing mentally has been shown to be very useful for developing athletic skills, and it works very well for any sort of skill.

There are a few things to consider when you prepare for this technique: Have the skill you want to develop clearly in your head. Find a *resource state* of confidence and success, which is to say, hold onto a feeling of confidence and success, and maybe even delight, throughout the process. Think of a place that would make the ideal setting.

For example, let's say you're trying to master the **skill** of doing tricks with a yoyo (don't laugh! Yoyo tricks are some of the most difficult things I ever attempted!). Decide in advance the tricks that you want to practice—know every step, and how they look and feel when you execute them perfectly. If you're not sure of one part, just work on the parts you do know. Don't forget to notice the proper timing, either.

Now choose the **feeling** that you feel when you do a really good job. That feeling that you feel when you do something you know very well. For some people they may choose a feeling of victory, for others they may want it to feel natural, so that they don't even think of it, like changing a light bulb. While you're at it, include a feeling of success. Even if you choose to make your yoyo trick feel so natural that you don't think twice about it, be sure you still reward yourself with a sense of satisfaction and success at your skill. You deserve that.

Finally, choose the best **place** in all the world for you to practice. Is it the Universal Super Yoyo Championship in Norway? (I just made that up). The Mayan pyramids in the Yucatan? A party where everyone is in awe of your skill? Pick the place that really works best *for you*.

Let's put it together:

1) Find a place to sit comfortably for a few moments and relax. Close your eyes.

2) Imagine your ideal place to practice. Really see it, hear the sounds, smell it, feel what it's like.

3) Get into your resource state—confidence and satisfaction, or whatever works best for you.

4) Now find yourself, feeling those feelings of your resource state, in your ideal location.

5) Begin to practice the skill in your mind. Do it, repeat it. Repeat it again. Each time you repeat it, begin to be more aware of all of the separate things you have to do: the movements, the feelings, the timing. Imagine yourself doing it perfectly. Repeat it each time, but in your mind, as if you were really doing it. If you want to move your body along at the same time, go ahead (make sure you have enough room to move freely and safely). Practice it over and over again, and notice any particulars that you may not have considered before.

6) As you repeat, change your perspective. Imagine you are now outside your body, looking at yourself practicing. Is there something you can see when you look at yourself, something that you didn't notice before? Are your feet in the right place? Your hands? Your timing? Correct anything that you feel needs correcting, until you're doing it perfectly. Be your own coach.

7) Go back into yourself, and make any changes you feel necessary. Notice if it feels any different. Repeat steps five and six until you feel great about it.

8) When you're done with that skill, if you have another one to practice, go on to that one. When you're done, imagine finishing, and putting away your equipment. Notice how really good you feel about yourself. How much you've accomplished. Give yourself a pat on the back. You deserve it.

9) When you're ready, open your eyes and shake out your limbs.

You'll be surprised that after just a little while, you will see improvements. You may also notice new ways to improve yourself that you never noticed before. I have used this for sports, and I can testify that it really works!

VARIATION C—FOR A SPECIFIC EVENT

Do you have a job interview, an exam or maybe a date coming up, that you'd like to be more prepared for? If you were an actor, you'd rehearse for a play. You life is your play, why not be as well-rehearsed?

Getting ready: As with the above technique, you have to know the setting, or the **place**, at least roughly. If you're going to an important interview, you may not know what the office will look like, but you do know there will probably be a desk and chairs, and maybe some papers, all the rest doesn't really matter.

Choose the best possible **feeling** to have in the situation. Confidence and authority in a job interview, charm and humor for a date, relaxation and accuracy for a test.

Finally, think of the **skill** you'll need. In this technique, the focus is on the particular event, but you'll still need to have your skills ready. For example, in the interview, you'll probably need your wits about you, to be able to field any question that they throw at you; if it's a date, you want to be able to create a feeling of romance and connection; and for the test, you want to exercise your fabulous total recall of facts.

1) Sit down, get comfortable and relax. Close your eyes.

2) Imagine yourself becoming energized. Really feel energized. Excited, as if anything were possible (it is!).

3) Now feel that specific **feeling** that you picked for this situation—confidence, authority, romance, humor, etc. Really feel that feeling, and hold onto it.

4) Imagine the **setting**. If it's the interview, imagine the desk, the chairs. If it's a date in a restaurant, imagine the table and chairs and lighting. See it, hear the sounds in the environment, feel the texture of the things with your fingertips.

5) Imagine the interviewer or your date, or the test in front of you. Imagine you're there too, still feeling the best possible feeling, and energized enough to act confidently and appropriately. Enjoy your energy, calmness, and coolness.

6) Now begin the show, see what's happening as if it's a movie you're starring in, and notice how very **skilled** you are. Notice the way you get the kind of results you want, that everything just falls into place for you. You handle everything in the best possible way, and the other people in the scene, if there are others, are

surprisingly compliant. Everything is working so very well for you. Be aware of how successful you are.

7) Notice anything you didn't notice before. Is there anything you want to improve? Are there any obstacles that might occur? If you were to rehearse solutions for those obstacles, what would they be?

8) Repeat the scene a few times and notice how much more smoothly everything goes. Be aware of improvements you can make.

9) Now imagine stepping outside of yourself, and observe it all from the outside, starting at the beginning. Is there anything you see that you didn't before?

10) If you want to make any changes, go ahead and try them out, seeing them from inside yourself and outside of yourself, until you really like what you see. When you're done, feel a sense of approval and give yourself a pat on the back. Feel free to rehearse in different ways and adjust for the best possible outcome.

11) Come back to the moment in your own time. Notice any insights, but don't over-analyze.

Skill, feeling, and **place**—the three important elements for an effective guided meditation.

Once you're clear on the skill or ability you want to exercise, and know the outcome you want, even if it's just a little mental rest & peace, you choose the feeling that will be the most appropriate, and create a setting. Then step in and enjoy! Explore! Be as successful as you want to be. Explore different outcomes until you find what feels best. This is a very good way to install new, positive beliefs.

There are even people who feel that when you strongly imagine specific outcomes in your life, you can actually manifest those changes in your life. There's so much material about that out there, under the heading of Law of Attraction and Manifestation, that I won't say more about it here. But if you're feeling game, give it a shot!

One more thing—when you're imagining to improve something in your life like a specific outcome or ability, it's important to take **action!** Follow it up by *doing* *something!* Mind and action together are an unbeatable combination. Some people even say that's all there is in the universe: mind and action. Sometimes, you find an immediate difference, other times it may take a little while before you see a difference, but inevitably you will begin to notice improvements.

Chapter 14
Standing meditations, moving meditations, and living meditations

Maybe you know someone who really loves their work—there's nothing they'd rather be doing, and it gives them a sense of excitement and a sense of peace. (Mind you, I'm not talking about those guys who love their job even though it gives them ulcers.) Maybe you'd like to be one of those people, to a reasonable degree? If you really love what you do, you'll find enjoyment comes pretty naturally, but there's no reason your knowledge of meditation can't improve whatever you're doing now. Meditation can be integrated into every aspect of your life, if you want to.

Is it possible that not everything you're doing right now is satisfying, or even worthy of you? If you're doing something right now that you simply have to do, being able to neutralize any of the negatives that go with it, like feelings of resistance or frustration, can help you flow through those things until you evolve on to doing something even better.

If you are doing something you enjoy already, making a meditation out of it can make it even more enjoyable, and maybe even help you be more efficient. If you find yourself having to do something that you don't enjoy, you may find these techniques can make things more satisfying.

By allowing yourself to relax any part of your body and mind that is non-essential to your task, and keeping your focus on the task at hand, as well as the final outcome you want, you can do amazing things for your skills and abilities, and it works hand-in-hand with the more traditional sitting types of meditations.

There's probably no physical endeavor more classically connected to meditation than Asian martial arts, and here's my take on why that synergy is there, and why it's been so successful.

Most martial arts are anything but placid and peaceful. Kicking, punching, screaming, stabbing, breaking bones, strangling and crushing hardly seem like activities that are conducive to a placid and stress-free mindset. One of the common explanations is that all of that violence requires an equal amount of peace and meditation to balance out the mind and body, the Yin and Yang philosophy, and that's certainly true, but there are deeper elements, too.

Surprisingly, there's a meditative element to the practice of fighting and training itself. Think about what is involved in a fighter's activities. An exchange of punches, kicks, or sword-cuts may take place in a fraction of a second, and that fraction of a second may be the difference between life and death (or crippling pain and injury). Pretty stressful business, huh? It's vitally important for a trained fighter to be able to **focus completely** on making his attacks and defenses successful with the most efficiency and the least wasted effort. He needs to be able to tune out distractions but still allow his subconscious to be aware of everything around that may influence the outcome of a fight, like the direction of the sun in his eyes, and the ground underfoot. Can you think of any of the meditational practices we've covered in this book that might be of value for that situation?

Training is an equally important issue to a fighter, and mind still plays a very important part in it. Imagine a karate student who wants to develop a really effective punch. In order to do so, he'll have to practice it thousands of times until it becomes a natural part of his neurology, and repeat it even more to develop power & physical efficiency. At the same time he's training his body, he has to train his mind for a certain emotional intensity—it's not enough that he can do the punch when he's practicing in the gym, it's important that he have the emotional focus so that he can do it in a fight effectively.

You may not be a kung fu fighter, but I'm betting that there are times that a meditative calm would benefit you in some way. Times when you're under stress, and keeping a clear and open head would benefit you incredibly. Maybe on the job, maybe in a ticklish family situation, maybe in some situation that's unique to you.

Standing and active meditations are the transition from sitting meditation to action meditation. When you're sitting, you have total control over all the stimuli that comes to you. Standing meditations are a step towards integrating that meditative state in a physically demanding situation.

Let's give it a try!

MEDITATION 20—STANDING TECHNIQUES

This meditation will be very much like the techniques that you know so well by now. Only the body position is different, but see what kind of a difference it makes.

Find a quiet place where you won't be disturbed for a few minutes. The light should not be distractingly bright, and there shouldn't be much distracting scenery in front of you. Standing, facing a wall or a calm landscape is ideal. (The first time you do this, try it for three minutes, take a rest and see how you feel).

You can close your eyes if you want to. Stand up straight, with your feet about shoulder-width apart, or whatever is natural and comfortable for you. You should be able to keep your weight evenly balanced on both feet with your legs straight but not stiff. Allow your arms to hang comfortably at your sides. Keep your back straight, your shoulders back and your head up, as if there were a string tied to the top of your head pulling your back up straight.

Stance 1: Standing   Be sure you're not slouching!

Once you've gotten comfortable in this stance, relax. Spend a few moments exploring the way your body feels in this position. Notice what your legs are feeling, your feet, your hips, your back, your shoulders, neck, head. Are there any places you feel tension? Relax everything as much as you can and still stand up straight. Notice the muscles of your face and if you find any tension there, relax that, too. Our goal in this stance, and all the other standing postures, is to relax everything as much as you can while still maintaining your stance uncompromisingly. Be aware that while you're doing the meditation you will notice things in your body. Tensions may arise while you're standing, and you will have to adjust while standing without pausing.

You should be experiencing a *physical stillness* at this point. This quality continually improves with time and practice.

Now, breathe in naturally and easily. Breathe in slowly, hold it for a moment, and exhale equally as slowly as you inhaled. Repeat.

After three minutes, take a deep breath, open your eyes wide, sit down and see how you feel. Do you notice anything different? Did you notice anything while you were standing?

At your own speed, and as your time allows, extend the amount of time you spend doing this standing meditation. You may find that as you continue, your breath will deepen, your limbs will relax, and your sense of balance will increase. Try it with your eyes open and with them closed. Notice whether there is a difference? Try it and see!

VARIATIONS:

Notice that this is basically **Meditation 1**, the breathing meditation, only the body position has changed. If you're doing one of the other meditations, and you've gotten to the point where you can quickly reach your desired meditative state, try it while standing. Most of the previous meditations will work: Mantras (**Meditation 12)**, or concentrating on an internal sound (**Meditation 9**), or holding an image in your mind (**Meditation 10)**, to name just a few.

Can you see how this standing meditation might help you to integrate your calm centeredness into everyday life? How about standing on the bus, or a quiet moment at the office? In a long line at the post office? I almost guarantee that opportunities will present themselves. If you can do it you're well on your way. As long as you're having fun experimenting with this, you will get it. Of course, when you're out there, keep your eyes open.

POSTURAL VARIATIONS

Spend a lot of time in one posture before you begin to experiment with others. I'd recommend about 6-8 weeks just in the first standing posture before you try a different one. If you do want to explore other stances, remember to begin with stances that allow you to keep your weight balanced on both feet, and the rest of your body as relaxed as possible without compromising your posture.

STANCE 2:

Just like the basic stance, but *put your heels together*! Doesn't sound very different, eh? Try it! This will make you much more aware of your own body, and your balance mechanism. It WILL be more of a challenge to most people.

Stance 2: Standing

STANCE 3:

The famous martial arts "Horse Stance" is called "Ma Bu" in Chinese. It's called the horse stance because it looks as if you should be riding a horse, with your legs wrapped around the animal. This stance will also develop your leg muscles. If you're a fighter, your legs are "the horse" you ride in a fight, so this stance also strengthens your own "horse." It can be a little rough on the knees, so be careful and begin gently.

Stance 3: Ma Bu

ASSUME THE STANCE LIKE THIS:

From a standing position, step to one side, perhaps 30-36 inches apart, or double the width of your shoulders. Both feet should be parallel to each other, toes pointed forward. Sink your weight slightly, push your knees outward a bit, tuck your hips slightly under you (push the pelvis forward a bit) and keep the back straight. Extend your arms in front of you, with your palms facing your chest and your arms rounded, as if you're holding an imaginary beach ball. Thumbs up, elbows pointed outward. To the Chinese, this is considered to exercise your lung meridian, to encourage your relaxed breathing. Keep your head up and *relax*! Hold it for three minutes the first time. Martial artists may hold this for up to half an hour in order to stay calm while in stance.

STANCE 4:

On one leg? Yes! You can do it! And you do it like this: Stand comfortably with legs slightly apart, the way you did in the original stance. Relax. Extend both arms straight out to your sides, shoulder high, palm up. When you're ready, slowly raise one leg. Let the knee stay bent. Raise your leg as high as you are comfortable doing so. Then hold it. Try it for two minutes, then slowly put your leg down, gently shift your weight, and raise the other leg. Hold that for two minutes. Don't forget the meditation basics: Breathing, calmness, openness, and awareness.

Stance 3:
Standing on one leg

MOVING MEDITATIONS

Once you're comfortable applying your meditational basics, there are a lot of directions you can take this.

Walking is the most obvious next step. Find a calm location where you can walk in a straight line for a while without having to worry about people or things around you. A quiet green in the park is great, or a beach, or an empty room. Begin by standing (**Meditation 20**), and once you're feeling calm and centered, begin to place one foot in front of the other. Be aware of your breathing. Often, it will begin to synchronize with your steps after a while. Don't focus on any one particular thing (**Meditation 15**), just take it all in. experiment with feeling, hearing, and seeing all while walking.

OTHER COMMON KINDS OF MOVING MEDITATION

Hatha Yoga is a system of physical exercise that increases your strength and flexibility while maintaining your meditational mindset. Many of the stances provide problems that have to be solved meditationally. Stretching, for example, requires a meditative realization in order to do it successfully.

If you don't have time or inclination to learn Yoga, a few good **stretching** positions will challenge you in a similar way. Passive, static types of stretches, the kind where you hold the stretch and gradually increase the stretch as you breathe and relax, have a natural yogic kind of calming effect. For example, the stretch covered earlier in the book, **touching your toes** (p. 35). You can bend forward and simply allow your weight to go forward as far as it comfortably will go. After holding the pose for a few seconds, the muscles will become accustomed to it and begin to relax, and as they relax, they'll begin to stretch. Gravity will naturally help, and all you have to do is breathe in a relaxed manner. There are so many different stretches you can do, and so many books and web pages on stretching, that you can find some that will be just right for you.

Tai Chi is a classical system of Chinese martial arts that emphasizes relaxed, continuous motion. There are several different styles, from Yang, which is more upright, to Wu and Chen, which are physically more demanding. They also have partner exercises called "push hands" that two people do together, which require relaxation, sensitivity, and awareness all at the same time. It's also a lot of fun!

Weightlifting doesn't really seem very Zen, but it requires an awful lot of mental focus and intensity. Regular practice is definitely meditative.

Karate. I touched briefly on the kinds of focus that "hard" martial arts (unlike Tai Chi, which is "softer") require. If this path appeals to you, go for it!

Juggling! Not classically a meditation, but it will require an amazing amount of focus just to learn it, and even after you've internalized the motions, it has a wonderful, relaxing quality to it.

Maybe you're starting to see ways you can apply the principles of meditation in your own life. Any activities like the abovementioned ones are ideal, since they go through a cycle of learning and repeating until you've internalized them. In the cases of the above, once you've internalized one set of actions, you may to find yourself drawn to the next, slightly more complicated set, which will provide continued challenges to keep the practice fun.

You can integrate the meditative process into the activities that you may have been taking for granted. Those activities you have to do every day, perhaps repetitive ones, are ideal as meditations; find yourself being mindful of the details while relaxing at the same time. By just *allowing*, you can work with less stress, which automatically makes you more effective, and it's not uncommon to find insights presenting themselves if you don't look for them.

> I once was hired by an advertising agency to design and assemble packages and displays. I am a designer by trade, but I'd never really cut out or assembled these kinds of things before. Every place I'd ever worked at had specialists to do that work, but this place wanted me! Always up for a challenge, I took the job. It was a little bit tricky at first, but an awful lot of fun. I didn't know most of the techniques that I needed for assembling these, but I discovered when left alone to work with what I had, and by keeping my mind open to the possibilities, the methods began to present themselves—some of my own methods were better than the "real" ones. It was as if the need for a technique was teaching me. By focusing on what I needed to do, without getting frustrated, and keeping my mind open, I soon had developed ways to get the jobs done five to ten times faster! The president of the company was fascinated. He used to like to come and watch me work, because he'd been in the biz for 40 years and had never seen the kinds of approaches I used. He was sure he was witnessing secret techniques. I never told him that I didn't know the 'right way' to do it. Just working from a calm, mindful state, and letting my needs dictate the approach, did the trick.

> Thomas Edison holds a whopping 1,093 patents. Many of them were created by his employees, to be fair, but he did design his fair share of them, and he was famous for his inspired problem-solving. It's been claimed that one of his favorite problem-solving techniques was to sit in a chair, thinking about his problem, until he dozed off. While he was sitting, in his hand he'd be holding a big ring of keys. At the moment he dropped off to sleep, he'd drop the keys, and the noise would jolt him

> to wakefulness. He'd write down whatever thought was in his head at the moment he awoke. Surprisingly often, the thought that came from his dream would be the inspiration he needed.

CREATIVE ACTIVITIES

I have been **drawing** for my entire life, at least from the time I could pick up a crayon and find a wall before my mom found me. Before I ever tried meditation, I'd already been spending a lot of time in drawing classes, literally hours trying to draw something in front of me, a flower, a statue, a live nude model. Typically the classes I was in were four hours long, and broken into 25-minute segments with a five-minute break in between, Drawing is powerfully calming, centering, and relaxing. It requires total focus and concentration, and I like to describe it as running a comb through your brain, because that's how you feel after a class: untangled. Mind you, there are moments of frustration, where nothing seems to be working, but eventually you sort those out, and you learn new strategies for dealing with frustrations. Ultimately, it transports you to a mindset where it's all you. You're trying to convert something you see into an image on paper, and it almost doesn't even matter what the thing is you're drawing. It's oddly exciting, and amazingly satisfying, even when the drawings don't quite work out. It's also interesting that one of the things you have to learn is how to get your mind out of your own way, just as we talked about in **Meditations 2, 3, and 4**, clearing the mind. Very often, especially when you're first starting, part of your mind will suggest ways you should draw a thing that just don't look right on paper. With practice it begins to come together, and you can always continue to get better.

Music offers so many opportunities to calm and focus the mind. Playing an instrument is naturally meditative in just the way drawing is, and if you're composing, it's a whole other creative, satisfying (and occasionally frustrating) endeavor.

Even *listening* to music can offer excellent benefits. Music, by its nature is like a guided meditation. Choose music you like, relax, and see where it can take you. Classical music is, well, classic, for this activity, but any music that makes you feel the way you want and captures your imagination, and hopefully expands your awareness, is excellent. Exciting music will pump up your energy levels and your mood, and contemplative, calm music will help relax your mind. Be careful of listening to negative music, or music with negative messages in it, since these will affect your mind. Aside from classical music, jazz, blues, instrumental, and world music are all great. Enjoy, and don't be afraid to try new things.

Chapter 15
Strategies for keeping your cool

In this book, we've talked a little bit about "stress." Now let's talk about it a little more. We know that stress affects just about everybody in our modern society, and there's no shortage of information about the effects of stress on a person's health. There's a huge industry based on helping people cope with stress: vitamins, herbs, essential oils, exercise programs, tapes, CDs, books, videos, spas, massage, saunas, mud-baths, diets, medications, therapies, candles, and that's just touching the surface. We know when we're stressed (although some people are so accustomed to living in stress that they've grown accustomed to it now), and we usually know what's stressing us out. But what exactly is stress? Let's take a look.

STRESS

The "fight or flight" response is the way a person's physiology responds to something in their environment that puts them on alert, a perception of a threat or a danger. The body reacts by releasing adrenaline, which also causes the muscles to tense and the blood pressure to rise. There's even an almost subconscious urge to action, to *move*, to *do something* now!

Physically, stress could be considered to be the tip of the fight or flight response.

But wait. Remember the last time you were really excited about something good, whether it was going on a trip, getting on an airplane, or going on a date with someone you really like. Wasn't there a pleasing, tingling rush of energy and excitement, an adrenaline release? Your blood pressure increased, your muscles tensed, maybe an exciting feeling of danger, and something inside you said *lets go, now!*

What gives? Physically, wasn't that the same kind of reaction as stress: nervousness, tension, and urge to act? If that's the case, why doesn't stress feel like fun? Stress and excitement are virtually identical physically, right? Well, remember back to the first part of this book, when we talked about motivation (**chapter 2**)? We said one kind of motivation is about moving *away from* punishment, while another is moving *towards* a reward? There's a clue there. When you're excited, you want to go *towards* the thing that excites you, but when you're stressed, you'd like to get *away from* the thing that's stressing you. Let's go a little deeper: *why is that?*

You might say that in one case you are preparing to escape from an overwhelming danger, that's the *flight* part, but in the other, you're readying to face dangers, because there's a reward worth fighting for at the outcome. That's the *fight* part of that equation. Consider also, when you're excited, you're generally the one initiating action, taking charge, but when you're stressed you're generally responding. You don't feel you're in control of the action.

Moreover, when you're not under stress, your expectations are generally congruent with the situation. You're stepping into a situation where you know, to some degree, what the final outcome should be, or at least that you're going to like it, while stressful situations are either ones where you are reacting and don't really feel you can control what's going on, and/or that when it's done you won't like the outcome.

Imagine that you're in your car driving down a road to get to your destination. You haven't been there before, but you have a good map to follow, and all the roads are clearly marked. You're able to judge how far to go and about how long the trip will take. When you arrive at your destination, it looks just the way you expected it to. No worries. Now imagine the scenario a little bit differently. You start the trip in your car, with the map, but as soon as you're underway, you find that the map doesn't match the roads. Some have different names, there are unexpected turn-offs, and it seems to be a lot farther than the map would indicate. Stressful? What if the traffic is also bad and you're not sure if you have enough gas to go all the way. Stressful now? What happens when you reach the destination and it doesn't look at all like what you expected? How will that make you feel?

When things in your life don't seem to be corresponding to your expectations, either in that moment or in the forseeable future, you get stressed. Moreover, that discrepancy can be the result of things not corresponding to *past patterns*, either. Past experience can set up certain expectations for future results. When things go as expected it feels good, but when the outcome deviates from expectations in some way, you are forced to react in ways you never did before, and that can be stressful ("It never used to go like this!"). Think about it: what are some of the things that have stressed you out? Getting an unexpected bill? Worrying that your vacation may not go the way you expected it? Discovering that your workplace suddenly instituted a new system and you have to do the same old thing in a whole different way? Or perhaps using the same tools you always do but finding they don't work the same way?

Any one of these things would make a good trigger for a stress reaction. Do you remember back in **Chapter 3**, when we talked about how a part of the mind is resistant to change because it wants to keep you safe, since it perceives any change as a potential threat to your safety? When that part of your mind perceives these changes beginning to occur, or when you have a reasonable expectation that they will, some part of you decides that you have to act NOW to correct things, and to act fast, before bad becomes worse.

You can probably also see now how meditative practices can be powerfully stress-relieving, since they take you fully into the "now" for a little while, and away from all of those future, present, and past inconsistencies that can make you chafe.

If you've been practicing your meditations for a while, you're starting to feel the benefits. Centeredness, calmness, and open awareness are becoming more familiar to you. But no matter how good you feel, there are still some situations that you can't control. You can't always avoid traffic jams, crowds, business, annoying people, relatives, loud children, rotten food, smoke…. And sometimes the more you try to hold onto your calmness, the more annoyances life throws in your face.

Stressful situations can just pounce upon you unawares, but more often, there's a sequence to the event. When it happens, try to break down the sequence. Think of the last stressful situation you were in. At first glance, you probably remember only the moment of greatest stress. But try to see it from a little farther removed, the "bigger picture," if you will. Very likely, there was a *before, during,* and *after* phase to it. Let's break down how you can use these three phases to your advantage when dealing with a stressful situation.

Before: Were you able to see trouble coming? Did you ever have a similar set of experiences in the past that might have warned you? Maybe you had an intuition? You can't always know when to expect the hammer to fall on you, but experience can give you clues as to when trouble is likely to occur again. Don't expect trouble, but if there's a possibility that there might be trouble down the road, it doesn't hurt to have a plan. One of my favorite sayings goes: "expect the best, but be prepared for the worst."

During: This is the part where it's as bad as it gets. When you're in the midst of a difficult situation, stay cool! No matter how bad it is, it won't go on forever. Panic gets you stuck in the moment, like a deer in the headlights, and makes it harder to move past it to the solution. The solution is the only thing that counts. Focus on that solution. Keep your eyes on the prize!

After: Don't dwell on the problem. Especially, don't dwell on the difficult emotions that came with it. If it's a problem that involved other people, remember that in times of stress, the best and the worst in people comes out. If there was "drama," leave it behind with the problem and move forward to the solution. *Do* study the problem so it doesn't happen again, and so that you can add to your toolbox of strategies for handling similar situations. The best way to study past difficulties is to do it without the emotion.

IN IT OR OUT OF IT?

The most touted benefit of meditation is that it gives you an ability to keep cool and not get swept up in the emotional tide. You may have heard of someone praised for doing something difficult with "Zen-like detachment," or having the "cool of a Buddhist monk," or even "needing the patience of a saint." You could even say that there's an almost holy quality to patience and calm. Happily, it's within our reach. In stressful situations, emotions flare, and it's very easy to allow your emotions to get out of your control. Now, when your emotions become controlled by your surrounding situation, the overall tide of energy becomes that much stronger, particularly if other people are involved, and that takes your control of yourself away from you. Isn't that the root of all stress—not being in control of yourself? Think about it for a minute. When other people's decisions steer your life, when you're not allowed to exercise your own best judgment, doesn't that create a gnawing feeling in your gut?

That gnawing feeling isn't good for anybody. On an individual level, it affects your health and your relationships. On the bigger scale, it can make or break nations. I think that same gnawing feeling was at the root of America's founding fathers' need to declare independence from England for the sake of "life, liberty, and the pursuit of happiness."

Keeping centered, keeping your cool in a crisis, is a wonderful trait to have. It lets you extract yourself from the crisis, to detach from it, and see the bigger picture, so you can respond in the best way. Detachment can definitely be an asset. It's an important skill to have when you need it, but at the same time, it's not a good state to be in all the time, unless you're living in a monastery. The meditational practices in this book will help you develop control over yourself and help develop the ability to get *in* and *out* of a state of detachment, to see clearly and without emotion when you need it.

Detachment is a great way to see the bigger picture clearly and choose the right action, but it's not a good substitute for *action*. Some people become detached when stress gets to be too much and they become inactive. But without action, it's unlikely the situation will change. Remember my original discussion of Yin and Yang, the two opposites? If detachment and inaction are the Yin, desire and action are the Yang, and you need both. And I did say *desire*. Desire fuels action! To the same degree that some people get into trouble by acting inappropriately, so, too can inaction be inappropriate at times. Don't be the deer int the headlights!

Develop control over your feelings and emotions, just don't go too far and allow yourself to become emotionally detached. Don't become numb to outside desires and emotions, and don't let them control you, either. It's a common saying in meditation circles to say "you must stamp out all desires," but that phrase needs a little clarification. It's the desires that make life worth living. Your desires give you direction in your life. You merely want to stamp out the control that the desires have over you, and instead use your abilities to have control over your desires. That way, you get to choose.

Even in a crisis, be able to step back enough to see the big picture, just don't become withdrawn, or you won't be able to take the action you need to change your world. Exercise reasonable caution, of course. Sometimes a situation becomes too severe, and it may be worthwhile to get out of there.

The reason I've included meditations on different kinds of sensory input and feelings is because it is through the senses that you engage your world and so it's good to have the opportunity to develop the senses, too, rather than just withdrawing from them. I think this is particularly important in our sometimes highly-charged society. Many Eastern techniques come from Confucian-based cultures that can be more emotionally restrictive than Western cultures. In those cultures, emotional detachment is a more expected trait, and even a desirable one. However, in the 21st century, even that is changing. As Asian cultures become more Westernized, people are becoming more emotionally expressive there, too. In any case, becoming disassociated from emotions is certainly not ideal in Western society.

BE FLEXIBLE

It's not enough to be able to step out of a crisis mentally and see all the ramifications if you're still locked into one single way of dealing with it. In order to find the best solution to a problem, you have to be flexible. In any situation, there's more than one way to achieve a solution. Some will be better than others, some are obvious and others hidden. You know enough ways now to avoid "brain-lock" when you're in a pinch. Use them and be able to adapt. Whether you're a boxer in the ring, a brain surgeon, or a mom negotiating through a crowded supermarket, the ability to see yourself and your outcome clearly, and all the ways to connect the two, will help you come out on top.

Uncertainty is a big stress-inducer, and in order to be prepared for it, some people will create rules in their life or their work. It seems to make sense: an uncertain situation comes up, and you have a rule to deal with it. For some things that works very well. It's easy and effective to have rules about driving in bad weather. For example, you could say: always have your headlights working, your seat belts on, and snow tires ready. We can make rules for our own lives, too: never drink too much, don't talk to strangers, excersise regularly and eat right. Rules can streamline a lot of situations, and by creating rules, more experienced people can effectively share their experience through those guidelines to less experienced people. Imagine someone going to work on a construction site for the first time. The rules there, created by the more experienced workers, can help him avoid injury and even save his life. Rules can be a great defense against stress brought about by uncertainty.

Rules can also be a great cause for stress. When rules are too limited or confining, badly thought out or just inappropriate, they actually cause more trouble than they solve. Some people will react by fighting against the rules, and others will experience stress by trying to follow the rules even when they clearly don't work.

Some people have rules for themselves and the way they live their lives. No matter how well these rules work for them, trouble can arise when one person tries to extend their rules to another person who may have a different way of doing things. There are millions of examples of this. For example, everything from the way in the 19th century, that left-handers were simply forced to write with their right hands in school, to the kinds of conflicts that happen when different cultures come together. It's also very common for couples to experience conflicts of this sort when they first move in together. It all needs a little give-and-take.

The Taoists say flexibility is life, rigidity is death. Be flexible and live!

BE PREPARED: AN OUNCE OF PREVENTION IS WORTH A POUND OF CURE

With time and regular practice of meditation, you'll find that you have more patience, and little things that used to annoy you will bother you less.

It's not always possible to see trouble coming down the road. However, if you're in a situation where the same difficulties come up from time to time, with practice, you'll begin to notice the warning signs before they become real problems. Are there any situations in your life, past or present that might fit this description? Take a moment and think about whether there might be warning signs you may not have noticed before. By anticipating the difficulties, you can be prepared. Being prepared is one of the best ways to keep your cool.

> At one point, I was in charge of a big project at a major advertising agency. The work was for one of our multimillion dollar clients, one of the biggest financial advisory companies in the world. Part of the work was to place a weekly advertisement in a financial magazine. Because the written part of the ad included time-sensitive interest-rate quotes, it was never ready to e-mail to the printer until almost 5:00pm, and the printer's deadline was 6:00pm. We had roughly an hour, usually less, to compose the ad, and the printer was halfway across the country! Despite the tight scheduling, I never lost my cool, and we almost never had a problem with the deadline. I say almost, because my boss always went home at 3:00pm—except this one time. I was used to getting the work done, just me and the few people I worked with, but this time my boss stayed and wanted to see how we did it. She was nervous about working with this ad—this was for one of our BIGGEST clients! She kept checking over my shoulder and asking, "Is it ready yet? Is it ready yet?" And reminding me & my people, "We CAN'T mess up! We CAN'T fail!" She was making us all nervous, and my continued calmness was making it even worse for her. In fact, her nervousness became near panic as the deadline rode around. She was nearly shaking with panic by the time the ad was ready to send. She was already rehearsing failure, and probably thinking up her excuses (and ways she could blame me), while she demanded that somebody call the printer to "stop the presses!" I reluctantly held back my laughter and pointed out solemnly that they wouldn't stop the presses for her or anybody. There was no stopping her now, either. She was almost fully into a panic attack. While she panicked, I finished the ad, and sent it to the printer. She was sweating with fear. If she had been actually involved in any part of the project besides observing, we'd never have made the deadline.

> Afterward, she said to me, "that was a VERY important client! We COULDN'T AFFORD to fail! We couldn't drop the ball! Didn't that bother you?"
>
> I calmly explained to her that eventually somebody WILL drop the ball, it's inevitable. And when it happens, we have another, "generic" ad stashed away, specifically for that client, which we can use instead. It didn't include the time-sensitive information, but it still advertised the client's services and kept their name in the paper, and it was only for emergencies (for the record, we never had to use it).
>
> When I told her that, I really thought she was going to faint.

Unless you're a brain surgeon, or a nuclear physicist, chances are that nobody dies when something you're working on flops. Unfortunately, short-sighted people can make little issues and deadlines seem a lot more critical than they really are in the big picture. For some, it gives them permission to panic. Hemingway used the phrase "the sun *also* rises" (my italics), for the title of one of his most famous books, but it also makes a good saying to stick on the fridge. No matter how dark it gets, the sun will always rise tomorrow. Nobody wants to screw up, but even if you're really doing your best job, and you really are good at it, you, or somebody close to you, WILL drop the ball from time to time. Don't fret, don't scream, don't die. Be prepared. When you or someone around you drops the ball, pick it up, dust it off, and run with it as best you can. Other times, when you're not under fire, take a minute and try to figure out exactly where it's possible to foul up *in the future*, and create a disaster plan, just in case. Like the old saying goes, an ounce of prevention is worth a pound of cure.

Remember, in the end, the guy who can stay calm under fire IS the hero who gets the job done.

Be aware that even though you can be prepared for trouble, it's not the same as rehearsing for trouble. Maybe you even know someone who fixates on difficulties. Rehearsing for trouble implies that you're expecting it to happen, and if you keep expecting it, odds are you'll eventually get it. Being prepared is like making sure you have a fire extinguisher in your kitchen. You choose the right kind, put it in the right place where you can reach it easily, but except for checking it occasionally to make sure it's fully functional, you don't think about it most of the time, and certainly don't dwell on it. You just know it's there if you ever do need it.

What if you're the one who fouls up? Well, I don't know what kind of situations you find yourself in, but I've never had a problem admitting when I made a mistake. Admitting it usually takes the attention off of finding the culprit and lets you put the attention on the important task of solving the problem. That's part of doing your best. If you've been doing a good job, no one should ever fault you for doing your best. People will usually appreciate someone who can see the solution and not just the problem. (Take that advice with a grain of salt, of course. Occasionally, you will be stuck dealing with someone who will fault you even for doing your best, so if that's the case, respond appropriately, so you're not putting your neck in the noose).

> First, DO look at the big picture to see how really important a thing is. Take it seriously, but put in perspective. Will the world end if it fails?
>
> Second, look at it in perspective: see how important it is to the people depending on whatever it is. Don't take their feelings lightly, but don't let their feelings influence yours so much you feel your control of yourself slipping.
>
> Third, be aware, when you can, of where failure can occur. Don't expect it, or focus on it, just be prepared for it if it happens. With you on the job, it probably won't, but you can't always tell. Simply be prepared.
>
> If things do fail, be honest about it, at least to yourself. Gently steer the attention of the people involved to the solution, and away from negative emotions. Focus on solutions, not problems.

WHAT'S THE PROBLEM?

What is your problem? Do you have a problem?

"Problem" is a really loaded word. Some people will start to feel a stress reaction as soon as they even read that word. *Problems? Oh, no!* Isn't there a feeling, like being backed up against the wall, when you think of having a problem? If someone set you up on a blind date with a beautiful stranger, and over a perfect dinner, they told you "I don't have any problems." chances are, for the rest of the night all you'll think of are "problems," and you'll be wondering what kind of problems your partner has that they're not telling you. It's a darkly powerful word. Problems at home? Problems at the office? *OH NO!*

The word "problem" has, for many people, an emotional component. There's nothing positive about a problem, and yet anything that can be considered a problem can also be described with other similar words. Roget's Online Thesaurus offers several interesting synonyms including: **complication, disagreement, dispute, question, pickle (!), brainteaser, example, grabber, illustration,**

intricacy, mind-boggler, mystery, puzzler, query, riddle, stickler, stumper, teaser, twister, and sixty-four thousand dollar question. Hmm. Interesting, isn't it? If you didn't actually read through the whole list, please do so right now, and notice the emotional connotations to those words. They can all be used in place of "problem," but they have subtle different meanings, don't they? Take a minute now, and think of the last problem you had to deal with, but as you think about it, try swapping one of the words from that list. Does your problem seem different if it were *a pickle?* How about brainteaser? A mystery? What if it's an illustration?

A lot of people find that by simply changing the words they use to refer to their issue, it changes the way they can deal with it. I mean, does anyone suffer real stress from a *brain teaser*? And if you find that words like dispute, complication or intricacy apply well to your particular "problem," you've also probably broken it down to a specific kind of a problem.

There are a couple of other words that people use to refer to their problems. Before I tell you the words, I'd like to tell you that the kind of people who use these words for their problems are usually highly successful people. The words they use are words like: **challenge, project, dare, tangle, venture, task**.

What if that problem were simply a *task*? Not so bad, now, is it? Just something you have to get out of the way. What if you were faced with a *challenge* instead of a problem? Not so bad, now? Maybe even exciting? Could you stand up to a *dare* differently than a problem?

If you've gotten used to dealing with your problems in a particular way, you might not be as aware of all the possible solutions available to you. A problem is like a hole you just want to get out of. But a challenge? A venture? A dare? Now, those are exciting, and something to be proud of solving.

Get into the habit of using positive words instead of negative ones like "problem," to deal with the issues that you have to face. Also get into the feeling behind those words: really see your issues as projects or challenges. Find creative ways of solving them, and look forward to honing your problem-solving skills. Don't get stuck trying to force a solution, but open yourself up to possible solutions you never thought of before, then evaluate the best of your options. When you can find options, it puts you more in control. It also gives you more flexibility. Mind you, it's not always easy to find creative solutions, in fact, it's a challenge, a skill that gets better with practice. The more you do it, the better it gets, and the better you get. If you've worked in an environment with a lot of other people, chances are, there's one there who generates problems more than solutions. They might even seem to have a sense of pride at their ability to accomplish...

nothing. Isn't it just more sane to devote all of that effort to doing something useful instead?

Words aside, get into the habit of approaching problems as a challenge or a project, too. Being able to "keep your head when all about you are losing theirs..." will definitely change the way you feel.

How do you eat an elephant? One bite at a time! If a task seems to be impossibly big for you, examine it to see how you can break it down into smaller, easy-to-handle pieces. Sometimes a problem can seem so big that you get paralyzed. Don't let yourself get stuck! As soon as a problem looks too big to handle, immediately start to look for ways you can break it down into littler pieces. Sometimes, a great big problem can be solved by just finding the one weak piece, but you have to look for it.

Try to define your problem with more precise language. "Problem" is a very generic word, almost a helpless one. If you examine the "problem" you're dealing with, and you find that it can be effectively described as, for example, a dispute, a complication, or a tangle, you'll find those terms are much more helpful. They will point you towards the solution. When someone hands you a "problem," grab your Sherlock Holmes magnifying glass and look at what it really is. If the problem is a *dispute,* that already hints at the approach you need: resolve the dispute. If it's a *complication,* you know there's something there that needs simplifying or explaining. If you're dealing with a *tangle,* unravel it!

And you know, this can apply to personal problems, too. If you're dealing with some sort of a "problem," how else could you describe it? How else could you think and feel about it? When a person has a personal issue, it's easy to get stuck in it. Changing the way you refer to it can open a lot of doors. For example, A lot of people who want to stop smoking start by defining their problem: "I'm a smoker." It seems like a straightforward statement, but on closer examination, there's a trap in it. If a person looks in the mirror and says "I'm a smoker," then what are they if they stop smoking? Now, if the same person looks in the mirror and says "I'm a person who smokes," it's a lot easier to give it up. It's the difference between *having* an issue and *being it.*

BE COOL

Stay cool. This is especially true if there's a person involved who's deliberately trying to make you lose your cool. Be aware that when people see you as strong and in control, some of them may become very jealous of you, and try to take you down a peg. Bratty children will sometimes test your limits, and so will some adults. If you begin to respond with emotion to their chiding, you've given them control over you, and that never feels good. It also sends a message to your detractors that they're succeeding in having power over you. Don't let 'em! As the athletes say, "never let 'em see ya sweat."

> Recently, I was sitting in the park, watching a woman with her little girl. She asked the child to do something, and the kid, being a kid, refused. Rather than keeping her calm and asserting herself with more calm and confidence, like a grown-up should, she immediately got angry. The child became more petulant, but you could see that the little girl had the reigns of control, and the angrier the mother got, the more resistant the child got. Soon the mother started screaming at the girl and the child grinned with delight and began running in a circle, with the mother in hot pursuit. The little girl was leading and the mother trailing behind. At that moment, Mom had handed over the keys to her life to a 3-year-old.

Anger and resistance only yield short-term results, and sometimes engender retribution. Since anger is by definition a *reaction* to something, control is in the hands of whatever or whoever caused the anger. Keep your cool.

A STITCH IN TIME

What happens when people panic? Typically, they get *so stuck* in the present moment that they cut themselves off from the past or the future, and the problem seems like it's all there ever was or will be. Has someone you know ever done this? Something undesirable happens, and they get totally tangled up in it, their entire mind gets absorbed by it. Remember nothing ever *just* happens, there's a past and a future. Like a piece of yarn with a tangle in it, it's not *just* the tangle. No, there's some yarn leading up *into* the tangle, and some yarn leading *out* the tangle. In the same way, some events led up to the catastrophe, and some events will get you past it. Don't get stuck in the moment! Examine the events that lead up to it, and see if there's something there you missed that might solve it.

Look past the "tangle" and see where it will lead. How can the damage be mitigated? Nothing is insoluble. Imagine looking forward into the future where the problem has already been solved in one or more different and satisfactory ways, and then work backwards to find and apply those ways.

THINK FOR YOURSELF!

Beware of the "group mind"! It's very easy to get swept away in the emotions of the mob. It may be half of the fun at a rave or a concert, or a Christmas party, but when the same gang is out of control, that may be a dance you want to sit out. It's very easy for downright silliness to seem like sense when everybody's emotionally inflamed, but it doesn't help resolve anything. There's a very real danger because mobs are ruled by passions and not logic. Another dangerous thing about the mob mentality is that the mob can quickly turn and become unified around the idea of finding a victim, for one reason or another. If it can't find its victim, it can turn on anyone, often, itself. In the time of the French Revolution, the revolutionary leader, Robespierre, sentenced hundreds to death by decapitation on the guillotine. Not so surprisingly, he ended up losing his head to the same guillotine himself, without a trial, when the wind of opinion changed direction.

You needn't go against the crowd, but don't surrender yourself to it, either, or you may find yourself doing things you'll regret. You're still responsible for the consequences of your actions.

TAKE A BREAK

Take some time off. I can almost guarantee that if you take a small break occasionally, even just three minutes, your precious problems will still be waiting for you when you get back. Remember that taking a break to collect your thoughts isn't the same as running away. You'll know when it's time to break, whether for five minute or a little bit more, if you find yourself continually making the same mistakes. It's kind of a sign. If it's a situation where others are relying on you, and don't think you can take a break, think of a way to collect your wits, even if it's just a five-minute bathroom break, and you'll be able to do a much better job when you've cleared your head. More people want you to succeed than fail, even if it's for their own selfish reasons, so they should understand. Sometimes it may be in everybody's interest to take a break for a minute.

Oddly, just the act of physically relocating away from the scene of the problem, even if it's only for a minute or two, can really take the pressure off, or even lead to the solution.

Always strive to maintain your perspective. As long as you don't let yourself get bound up in emotion, or tied to the moment, you should always have the freedom to see a question from different perspectives.

PATIENCE

A lot of people talk about the importance of developing patience. I haven't mentioned it outrightly before since it's hard to deal with the idea of patience while you're dealing with a situation, but you'll find it's woven, in one way or another, throughout this chapter and much of the rest of this book. All I'll say is, patience nets results!

In closing, a poem I've found worth studying, and maybe even memorizing, is "If" written by Rudyard Kipling in 1910. (Ladies, please forgive the 19th century chauvinism, and appreciate the valuable advice offered here in rhyme.)

If by Rudyard Kipling

If you can keep your head when all about you
Are losing theirs and blaming it on you;
If you can trust yourself when all men doubt you,
But make allowance for their doubting too:
If you can wait and not be tired by waiting,
Or being lied about, don't deal in lies,
Or being hated, don't give way to hating,
And yet don't look too good, nor talk too wise;

If you can dream—and not make dreams your master;
If you can think—and not make thoughts your aim,
If you can meet with Triumph and Disaster
And treat those two imposters just the same:
If you can bear to hear the truth you've spoken
Twisted by knaves to make a trap for fools,
Or watch the things you gave your life to, broken,
And stoop and build 'em up with worn-out tools;

If you can make one heap of all your winnings
And risk it on one turn of pitch-and-toss,
And lose, and start again at your beginnings
And never breathe a word about your loss:
If you can force your heart and nerve and sinew
To serve your turn long after they are gone,
And so hold on when there is nothing in you
Except the Will which says to them: "Hold on!"

If you can talk with crowds and keep your virtue,
Or walk with Kings—nor lose the common touch,
If neither foes nor loving friends can hurt you,
If all men count with you, but none too much:
If you can fill the unforgiving minute
With sixty seconds' worth of distance run,
Yours is the Earth and everything that's in it,
And—which is more—you'll be a Man, my son!

CONCLUSION

Thanks you for staying with me until the end! I've written this little tome to be of *use*. Try what you want and find what fits you best. Remember that nothing works for everybody, so if one technique isn't clicking, try another. You should be getting good results pretty fast. Don't continue with any technique that is making you feel more crummy, though. You'll be able to find more knowledgeable sources for deeper study of meditation on the Web, in libraries, and bookstores and from various other sources, as well as more formal schools and philosophies.

If you get benefit from this little work, please do tell people! There are no secret techniques here, just the best and easiest (in my opinion), and it's in the practice rather than the study that you'll find the potential for happiness.

If you'd like to contact the author, or get more information on updates newsletters, and courses related to this book, please visit:

www.21centurymeditation.info

and the blog at:
http://everybodymeditate.blogspot.com/

Now go forth, be brilliant, and be cool!

BIBLIOGRAPHY AND FURTHER READING

All of the following books are fairly easy to find, and offer an interesting variety of perspectives. There is a great deal of material on many different styles of meditation. A great deal of the most modern & accessible materials has been generated by Zen followers, and I've included some of the more insightful and entertaining ones here.

Meditation and Mindfulness
Ellwood, Robert, **Finding the Quiet Mind**, Quest Books (1983)
Top of the list, and incidentally, a great little book to start with!
Fields, Rick, **Chop Wood, Carry Water**, Tarcher (1984)
Kipling, Rudyard, **Gunga Din and Other Favorite Poems**, (Dover Thrift Editions) Dover Publications (1990)
Long, Max Fredom, **The Secret Science at Work**, Kessinger Publishing (2006)
Max Freedom Long spent a great deal of the first half of the 20th century reconstructing the Hawaiian belief system known as Huna, based on his extensive research and personal experimentation. What resulted is a powerful system of self-development, which is becoming more and more popular today.
Ramacharaka (Yogi), **Fourteen Lessons in Yogi Philosophy**, Yogi Publication Society (1904)
Ramacharaka (Yogi), **Raja Yoga or Mental Development**, Yogi Publication Society (1905)
Ramacharaka (Yogi), **Science of Breath**, Yogi Publication Society (1903)
Yogi Ramacharaka was the pseudonym of William Walker Atkinson, a very active voice of the New Thought movement of the early 20th century. Works on traditional Indian, or at least Indian-style, subjects were published under the name of Ramacharaka, works on New Thought were published on his own name. Some of his books were written over one hundred years ago, and many withstand the tests of time.
Reps, Paul, **Zen Flesh Zen Bones: A Collection of Zen and Pre-Zen Writings**, Tuttle Publishing (1998)
Reps, Paul, **Zen Telegrams: 79 Picture Poems**, Tuttle Publishing (1959)
Salajan, Ioanna, **Zen Comics**, Tuttle Publishing (1974)
Selby, John, and Selig, Zachary, **Kundalini Awakening: A Gentle Guide to Chakra Activation and Spiritual Growth**, Bantam (1992)
Suzuki, D.T., **An Introduction to Zen Buddhism**, Grove Press (1994)
Suzuki, D.T., **Essays in Zen Buddhism**, Rider (1958)
Watts, Alan, **Still the Mind: An Introduction to Meditation**, New World Library (2002)
Watts, Alan, **The Book: On the Taboo Against Knowing Who You Are**, Vintage (1989)
Watts, Alan, **The Wisdom of Insecurity**, Vintage (1968)

Watts, Alan, **This Is It: and Other Essays on Zen and Spiritual Experience**, Vintage (1973)
Alan Watts is one of the premier figures involved in the introduction of Zen to Western society in the 60s. His works are insightful and filled his signature dry, shall we say "Zen-like," wit.

Historical Material
There are a number of different translations of these currently available. Find one that appeals to you, and if you like it, read a different translation and see how similar and different they are, and what each can do for you. Every translator approaches the same material with his own particular point of view, and by reading more than one perspective, you can find some new insights.

Lao Tzu, Tao Te Ching
Tao Te Ching (also spelled Dao De Jing), puts down the precepts of the Taoist philosophy in poetic stanzas. Some are very straightforward, others become more comprehensible with continued reflection (and make excellent subjects for meditation themselves). Lao Tzu is an apocryphal figure, and the name actually means "old man" in Chinese.

Meditations of Marcus Aurelius
Marcus Aurelius was both a Roman emperor and a soldier. A great deal of his stoic thought was formed in the stark, life and death conditions of battle.

Meister Eckhardt (or Eckhart, Eckhard), Various sermons and writings
Meister Eckhardt was a medieval bishop who wrote and preached a very meditative, introspective approach to life, which was quite controversial for its time (or maybe any time!).

Neuro Linguistic Programming (NLP)
The rough organization of the techniques in this book based on different sensory experiences (visual, auditory, and kinesthetic) comes from one of the approaches utilized by NLP. NLP is primarily a series of therapeutic techniques based on the way the conscious and subconscious mind works garnered from a wide field of research and experience. One of the nice things about NLP is that it's grounded very strongly on empirical phenomena, that is to say, observable, repeatable experience, rather than being grounded in theory. NLP's approach to dealing with any issue is usually to start in the present, which in some ways corresponds to the approach of most meditational techniques.

Bandler, Richard & Grinder, John, **Frogs into Princes**, Real People Press (1979)
Bandler, Richard & Grinder, John, **Tranceformations**, Real People Press (1981)
Richard Bandler and John Grinder are two of the main founders of NLP. These

two books are some of the earliest books on the subject. They are entertaining to read, and full of useful techniques, but may require rereading to get the most out of them.
Steve Andreas, Charles Faulkner, **NLP: The New Technology of Achievement**, Harper Paperbacks (1996)

INDEX

Adrenaline	9, 115
Advertising	26, 97, 113, 121
Affirmation	69-72
Anchoring (a resource state)	39, 83-84
Auditory	11, 50, 53, 61, 132
Aunt Bertha	80
Back stretch	34
Barbados	59
Beliefs	13-17
Belly Chakra (Manipura)	85-87
Benson, Herbert	8
Blockages	85-88
Brain Frequencies, Alpha, Beta, Gamma, Delta, Theta	10
Brain, Left, Right	7
Break, Take a	127
Breathe, Breath	30, 33, 37, 41-43, 45-47
Buddhism	3
Candles	31, 57
Centeredness	22, 56, 81, 110, 117
Chakra diagram	86
Chakra	84, 85, 88, 95
Chest breath	41, 42
Chime	54
Christianity	4
Clock or timer	30, 31
Clothing	30
Conclusion	129
Cool (be)	80, 115-119, 121, 125
Corpse position	34, 94
Coué, Emile	70, 97
Creative activities	114
Cross legged	32, 33
Daydreams	95-96
Detachment	29, 118-119
Diaphragmatic (Belly) breath	42
Direction	19, 22
Drawing	114
Drugs	8, 32
Edison, Thomas	113
Emotion	iii, 8, 16, 22, 31, 41, 71, 78, 81-86, 89, 90
Empathy	94

Emptying your mind	89
Equipment	30, 54, 102
Feelings	8, 9, 88, 93-94, 119, 123
Fencing	61, 69, 70
Field of Vision Diagram	79
Fight or Flight	115
Flexible (be)	15, 120, 121
FOCUSING ON INTERNALS	60
Future Activities	82
Gaze	56, 77-79
Getting started	29
Glass	54, 64
Good & Bad criteria	14
Group Mind	126
Hand chakra experiment	84
Hatha Yoga	112
Heart Chakra (Anahata)	85-88
"Hercules, I am"	69
Hinduism	3
Horse Stance	111
"I am"	71
"If," by Rudyard Kipling	128
Incense	31, 56-57, 59-60
Inspiration	26, 74, 77, 83, 89, 91, 93, 114
Instrument	15, 53, 54, 114
Internal Dialogue	16, 26, 48, 50, 72
Intuition	26, 27, 75, 93, 94, 118
Islam	5
Journal	30, 46
Juggling	112
Karate	112
Kinesthetic	11, 132
Kyrie Elieson	71
Limitations	13, 15
Limiting Beliefs	13
Listening	27, 114
Little Voice	15, 16
Lying Down (corpse position)	34
Ma Bu	111
Mala or Rosary	25, 27, 30, 55, 69-73, 80, 110
Mantra	69
Marcus Aurelius	22

Martial Arts	108, 111, 112
Meares, Ainslie	8
Meditation 1—Breathing Technique	45
Meditation 2—Emptying the Mind of Sounds (Yin)	47
Meditation 3—Emptying the Mind of Imagery (Yin)	49
Meditation 4—Emptying the Mind of Sensations (Yin)	50
Meditation 5 (Variation)—Focusing on Om (Yang)	55
Meditation 5—Focusing on an External Sound (Yang)	53
Meditation 6—Focusing on an External Sight (Yang)	56
Meditation 7—Focusing on a Feeling (Yang)	57
Meditation 8— Focusing on a Smell (Yang)	58
Meditation 9—Focusing on an Internal Sound (Yang)	60
Meditation 10 (Variation A)—A Picture	63
Meditation 10 (Variation B)—Colors	54
Meditation 10 (Variation C)—Picture and Color Combined	65
Meditation 10—Focusing on a Visualization (Yang)	62
Meditation 11 Focusing on an Internal Feeling (Yang)	66
Meditation 12 (Variation A)—Repetition	72
Meditation 12 (Variation B)—Casual	72
Meditation 12 (Variation C)—Meaning	73
Meditation 12 (Variation D)—Prayer	73
Meditation 12—Focusing on a Mantra/Prayer (Yang)	72
Meditation 13 (Technique)	73
Meditation 13—Focusing on a Visualization (Yang)	73
Meditation 14 (Variation A)—Mirror	77
Meditation 14 (Variation B)—Smile	78
Meditation 14 (Variation C)—Confidence	78
Meditation 14—Focusing on a Mirror Reflection (Yang)	77
Meditation 15—Developing Peripheral Sight (Yang)	78
Meditation 16—Developing a Feeling/Resource State (Yang)	80
Meditation 17—Chakra Meditation (Yang)	84
Meditation 18—Emptying Your Mind (Yin)	89
Meditation 19 (Variation A)—Confidence and Comfort	97
Meditation 19 (Variation B)—Developing Personal Skills	101
Meditation 19 (Variation C)—For a Specific Event	103
Meditation 19—Breathing Guided Visualizations (Yang)	95
Meditation 20—Standing Techniques	109
Metaphor	50, 97
Metaphysics	93
Mind-Body Connection	10
Mind, Conscious, Unconscious, Subconscious	7
Mixed Breathing	42

Motivation: Towards and Away From	12, 116
Moving Meditations	111
Music	11, 60, 74, 114
Olympic Athletes	90
Om Mani Padme Hum	71
Om Nama Shivaya	71
Om	55, 60
One-legged stance	111
Past Experiences	83
Patience	118, 121, 127
Peripheral Vision Diagram	80
Personal Change	75
Physical Stillness	109
Pictures	73
Positions	32
Prayer	25, 27, 30, 71-73, 69
Prepared (be)	121-123
Problem Solving	89, 127
Problems	123-124
Psychometry	89, 95
Reading	2, 97
Relax	27
Relaxation Response, the	8
Research	8, 101
Resource State	80, 81, 101-102
Root Chakra (Mulhadhara)	85-86, 89
Rules	120
Scented Candles	32
Seating	32
Seiza	34
Self Exploration	83
Senses, The	10
Sensory Ranges	11
Sexual Chakra (Svadhisthana)	85-87
Shri Yantra	74
Sitting	32
Sitting in a chair	33
Skill, Feeling, Place	104
Sleep	10, 34, 50, 93
Stance 2	110
Stance 3	111
Stance 4	111

Standing	109
State-Dependant Learning	89
Stoic Philosophy	22
Stress	85, 96, 108, 113, 115-120
Tai Chi	112
Tangle	70, 124-125, 126
Taoism	4
Telepathy	94
Theosophists	56, 71
Third Eye (Ajna)	85-87
Thoughts	7, 8, 9, 26, 46-51, 70, 81, 90-93,
Throat Chakra (Vishuddha)	85-87
Tibertan Buddhism	3, 4, 10, 31
Top of Head Chakra (Sahasrara)	85-87
Trataka	56-57
Uncertainty	120
Visual	10, 11, 50, 62, 64
Visualization	62, 73, 74, 76, 80, 95, 97
Walking	112
Warning	29
Weight Lifting	112
Yin & Yang	25
Zen Buddhism	3

www.ingramcontent.com/pod-product-compliance
Lightning Source LLC
Chambersburg PA
CBHW032124090426
42743CB00007B/453